Humorous Incidents and Quips
for Church Publications

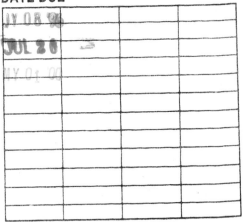

Humorous Incidents and Quips for Church Publications

Leslie B. and Bernice Flynn

BAKER BOOK HOUSE
Grand Rapids, Michigan 49516

9/95

Copyright 1990 by
Baker Book House Company

ISBN: 0-8010-3556-2

Printed in the United States of America

Bookstore

To
my lovely
humor-loving cousin
Betty Barram
and her gracious husband
Ed

Contents

Preface

My wife and I were listening to a speaker at the National Religious Broadcasters' annual convention in Washington, D.C. To make a point he told a story that brought a roar of laughter from the audience. I saw my wife take out her little notebook and write.

At a state denominational banquet at West Point Military Academy a young pastor told of a humorous event at his church. As I looked at my wife across the table, our eyes met and we nodded. This time I pulled out my notebook and captured the humorous anecdote.

At a library we looked through several secular humor books, getting a church-related joke now and again.

Coming home from a ladies' meeting, my wife told me another funny story.

The humorous incidents in this book are the result of years of enjoyable collecting. More incidents were discarded than included.

God meant us to enjoy humor. He gave us an environment with a touch of the comical. Who hasn't been amused by the antics of the monkey or the squeaky phrases of the parrot?

Humor can be a teaching device, clarifying, illustrating, and making truth more palatable. I had a pastor who said, "When I get people laughing over a well-placed joke, I pour a dose of truth into their mouths." Humor can relieve tension, recapture lagging attention, and even aid in the cure of illness.

Our prayer is that this collection of incidents may be as merry medicine to both your soul and body.

Leslie B. Flynn

Age

A reporter asked a man celebrating his one hundredth birthday, "What are you most proud of?" Replied the man, "That I've lived a hundred years and haven't an enemy in the world." Noting that the old man had a feisty nature, the reporter probed, "And how did you manage that?" Came the retort, "I've outlived every last one of them!"

Every morning a retired gentleman took a short stroll around his yard before starting his customary longer walk around several blocks. He explained to a curious neighbor, "It's the preamble to my constitution."

A talk-show celebrity, ending an interview with a member of a church's senior citizen's club, remarked, "I've enjoyed talking with you on your ninety-ninth birthday. I hope I'm around to talk to you on your one hundredth birthday next year."
Replied the senior citizen, "Why not? You look healthy enough to me."

The choir director had his picture taken, but was disappointed with the proofs. "I don't understand it. The last time I posed for you, the pictures turned out grand."
"Ah, yes," said the photographer, "but you must remember that I was ten years younger then."

A young executive refused employment to a senior citizen, "Because you're over the hill."

The senior citizen retorted, "That's better than being under the hill."

At a church social a visitor asked the pastor to guess her age. When he hesitated, she said, "Oh, you must have some idea."

"I have two ideas," he admitted. "My problem is . . . I can't decide whether to make you ten years younger because of your looks, or ten years older because of your charm."

Cautioning the witness to remember that she was under oath, the lawyer asked, "How old are you?"

"Twenty-nine and some months," she replied.

"How many months?"

"A hundred and ten."

A daughter asked her father who had just turned ninety, and who had never shown any fear of death, if now he did not have some fear of dying.

He answered, "I have no fears. Statistics prove that more people die under ninety than over ninety."

It's hard to say when one generation ends and the next begins, but it's somewhere around nine or ten at night.

The seven stages of a woman's life: *baby, child, junior miss, senior high, young woman, young woman, young woman.*

Confessed a fellow along in years, "I know I'm getting older. Even my dreams are reruns."

Somehow or other, as we get older work seems a lot less fun, and fun seems a lot more work.

Birthdays: Anniversaries on which the husband takes a day off, and the wife takes a year off.

When it comes to telling her age, she's shy—about ten years shy.

Middle age: The difficult period between adolescence and retirement, when you have to take care of yourself.

A retired gentleman said that he had come to understand the three stages of life: youth, middle age, and "You're looking well."

A sweet but seedy-looking, elderly man cashed his check at a supermarket. Gratefully squeezing the cashier's hand, he said, "I don't know how I'd get along without you people now that the bank has stopped cashing my check."

Animals

A summer Bible camp advertised all kinds of horses for all kinds of young people. "For tall youth we have tall horses. For short folks we have short horses. For slow people we have slow horses. And for fast persons we have fast horses." Then the ad went on, "Also, for those who have never ridden a horse before, we have horses that have never been ridden."

SUNDAY SCHOOL TEACHER: This is "Be Kind to Animals Week." Any of you done a kind deed to animals?
FOURTH-GRADER: I kicked a kid for kicking his dog.

Tom was disgusted when the phone woke him at two in the morning. Picking up the receiver, he recognized a neighbor's voice complaining, "Your dog is barking so loudly I can't sleep."

Next morning, at 2:00 A.M. sharp, Tom rang up his neighbor and calmly announced, "I just wanted you to know that I don't have a dog."

At a Sunday school department outing to the zoo, around 3:30 P.M. parents noticed a sign: CLAIM LOST CHILDREN AT LION HOUSE BEFORE 4 P.M. FEEDING.

Two caterpillars were crawling across the lawn when a butterfly flew over them. As they looked up at the beautiful fluttering creature, one nudged the other, "You couldn't get me up in one of those things for a million dollars."

A devoted teacher took her Pioneer Girl group to the Museum of Natural History. Her pupils enjoyed every minute of it. At dinner that evening one of the fathers asked his daughter, "Where did your group go today?"

Quick as a flash came the answer, "We've been to a dead circus."

The reason a dog has so many friends is because he wags his tail instead of his tongue.

Wouldn't the horse of a century ago have a good laugh if he could see all those motorists of today adjusting their shoulder harnesses?

Announcements

The concert in the lower auditorium last Friday night was a huge success. A special thanks to the pastor's daughter who labored the entire evening at the piano, which as usual fell on her.

The Diet Club will meet Thursday night at 7:30 P.M. Please use the large double door at the side entrance.

A family-type film, suitable for both children and parents, will be shown at the Sunday evening service at 6:00 P.M. Free puppies will be given to all children not accompanied by a parent.

Our annual church picnic will be held Saturday afternoon. If it rains, it will be held in the morning.

Antiques

A collector of old books ran into an old, but unschooled friend who said that he had thrown away an old Bible which had been in the family for generations. "Somebody named 'Guten something or other' had printed it."

"Not Gutenberg," gasped the book collector. "You threw away one of the first books ever printed. A copy sold for over four hundred thousand dollars last month!"

The friend explained, "My copy wouldn't have brought a dime. You see some fellow by the name of Martin Luther had scribbled his name all over it."

WOMAN: Our furniture goes back to Louis the Fourteenth.
NEIGHBOR: Ours goes back to Sears on the fifteenth.

When people looked surprised at meeting his young-looking wife, an older husband would inevitably remark, "My wife likes antiques. That's why she married me."

A tourist in Jerusalem asked, "Where will you find a modern building that has lasted as long as these ancient ones?"

Atheism

A Soviet teacher, trying to prove to her class that God did not exist, emphasized that the Soviet astronauts in orbit did not see him.
One seven-year-old suggested, "They fly too low."

An evangelist, handed a note by an usher just before the sermon, opened the folded piece of paper to find one word scrawled in large print: FOOL.
Rising to preach, the evangelist said, "I've just been handed a memo which contains the single word FOOL. I've heard of people writing letters and forgetting to sign their name. But this is the first time I've ever heard of anyone signing his name, and then forgetting to write the letter!"

An atheist complained to a Christian, "You Christians have all the holidays: Christmas, Good Friday, Easter, Ascension, Pentecost, Thanksgiving, and others."
The Christian retorted, "You can have April first."

President Eisenhower's definition of an atheist: A guy who watches a football game between Notre Dame and Southern Methodist and doesn't care who wins.

Bible

Little Robert wanted a watch so badly that he wearied the whole family with his begging. His father promised him a watch when he was older, then forbad him to mention the topic again.

Next Sunday during devotions at the breakfast table the children, as was their custom, repeated Bible verses. Little Robert astonished them all by quoting, "What I say unto you, I say unto all, Watch."

A son in Texas wanted to send his mother an unusual, expensive gift for Mother's Day. The owner of a pet shop told him of a Minah bird worth well over twenty thousand dollars, the only one in the world that could recite the Lord's Prayer, the twenty-third Psalm, and 1 Corinthians 13.

"I'll take it, " said the Texan. "I don't care how much it costs. Mother is worth it and will get so much comfort hearing it recite Scripture." So he wrote a check and had it shipped off to his mother.

The Monday after Mother's Day he called her long distance. "Did you get my present?"

"I certainly did, and thank you."

"And how did you like the bird?"

"It was delicious, Son."

A men's Sunday school class teacher, who had difficulty remembering names of Bible characters in his lessons, was advised to write those names on paper and pin the paper on the inside of his coat jacket. Next Sunday, trying to recall the names of Jesus' three inner disciples, he looked down inside his jacket, and exclaimed, "Hart, Schaffner & Marx."

A pastor received a letter from a long-time parishioner which read, "Dear pastor: If Jesus Christ knew what you are doing to our church, he would turn over in his grave."

Reading the letter to his board, the pastor commented, "It makes me wonder what her theological position will be—come Easter."

Explaining the various items in the Christian's armor, a Sunday school teacher said, "Another weapon we should carry is the Word of God. Can anyone remember what the apostle Paul called the Word of God?"

When no answer was forthcoming, he added, "It's something very sharp, something that cuts."

One little fellow chirped up, "I know. It's the axe of the apostles."

People who quote Scripture often quote only the parts they like.

TEACHER: Does anyone know where to find the Beatitudes?
BOY: Did you try the Yellow Pages?

After his first few weeks in Sunday school a boy said, "Daddy, I want to ask you a question. The teacher keeps telling us about the children of Israel as slaves in Egypt, the children of Israel crossing the Red Sea, the children of Israel in the wilderness, the children of Israel offering sacrifices. Didn't the grown-ups do *anything?*"

A young minister, ecstatic at the birth of a new baby boy, sent his mother this brief telegram: ISAIAH 9:6.

Mom read too much into the message. She telephoned her husband at the office, "A telegram came. Our daughter-in-law evidently had a boy who weighs nine pounds and six ounces, and they've named him Isaiah."

A pastor, teaching a communicants' class, asked a boy, "What is the Trinity?"

The boy who had a weak voice answered somewhat quietly, "Father, Son, and Holy Spirit."

Straining to hear, the pastor said, "I can't quite understand you."

To which the bright young lad replied, "You're not supposed to—it's a mystery."

A homiletics professor said to his seminary class, "Students, when you want an illustration for a sermon, take it out of the Bible. Your people will not be familiar with it."

A South Sea islander, writing to a friend about a great revival they were experiencing, said, "We are having a great rebible here."

The proprietor of a country store, who professedly ran his business strictly on biblical principles, would always quote a Scripture verse whenever he rang up a sale on the cash register. For example, if a little boy bought some candy, the owner would say, "Mark 10:14: Suffer the little children to come unto me and forbid them not." If he sold a customer an article of clothing, he would say, "Matthew 6:30: Shall he not much more clothe you, O ye of little faith?"

One day a stranger came in, looking for a particular kind of hat. When the stranger asked if he had a more expensive hat, the owner produced a hat which, though really the same price, he said was twenty-five dollars more. When the owner rang up the sale, and the customer departed, bystanders in the store wondered how the owner would fit this shady deal with Scripture. Finally he said, "Matthew 25:35: He was a stranger, and I took him in."

Bibles (Old English)

Explaining the verse in the Gospels about Jesus healing "sick people taken with divers diseases" (Mark 1:34), a preacher shouted, "There's a regular epidemic of divers diseases among us. Some dive for the TV set at the Sunday-evening service hour. Some dive for the car for a weekend trip, while others dive for their dimes and nickels to put into the offering. It takes the Lord and a love for the church to cure DIVERS DISEASES."

After Grandpa had some teeth pulled, he spoke with a lisp. His granddaughter listened curiously as he read his usual Bible story to her the first night after his visit to the dentist.

Hearing words like "saith" and "hath" and "doth," she exclaimed, "God had his teeth out, too!"

Boasting

A Pennsylvania citizen, arriving in heaven, was asked to share some experience from his earthly days. The new arrival jumped at the opportunity. "I survived the Johnstown flood of 1889. Over two thousand people perished in the destruction. It was one of America's worst disasters. I've told the story over and over. Now I can tell it up here."

"That will be fine," said his guide. "But remember—Noah will be out there in the audience."

A woodpecker in Louisiana was drilling away at a tree. Suddenly, a lightning bolt struck, splintering the tree into pieces. Miraculously unhurt, the woodpecker backed off, gazed at the mess, and then flew away. Returning with seven other woodpeckers, he said, "Look, fellows, there it is."

A Texas rancher, who owned a very large ranch, was talking to a farmer from another state who had only a modest farm. The Texan bragged about the size of Texas, and how everything was done on a large scale. Emphasizing the size of his ranch, he said to the farmer, "I got up this morning at sunrise and started driving across my ranch, and by noon I was only halfway across my land."

Nodding understandably, the farmer replied, "Many years ago I had a car like that, too."

A plane with pilot and three passengers aboard began to lose altitude, slowly but surely. The pilot told the others that only three parachutes were available for the four of them.

One man spoke up immediately. "I'm the president of my company. It's important for me to be saved." And he grabbed one of the parachutes.

Another man piped up, "I'm an inventor. I have brains. My intelligence is needed. I'll use a parachute."

Out went both of them. The remaining passenger looked at the pilot, quietly asking, "Which of us will take the last parachute?"

The pilot replied, "I still have two parachutes. The guy with the brains took my knapsack."

A boy, who bragged about his shooting accuracy, took his friend hunting. Aiming at a bird, and missing, he said to his friend, "There you see a miracle—a dead bird flying."

Every time he opens his mouth, he puts his feats in.

He who thinks he knows it all is most annoying to those of us who do.

When you try to make an impression, that's the impression you make.

Bulletin Board

(Outside a convent in California):
Trespassers will be prosecuted to the fullest extent of the law: SISTERS OF MERCY.

(During a minister's illness):
GOD IS GOOD.
Dr. Jensen is better.

(Announcing a special musical presentation during the pastor's summer vacation):
NO SERMON SUNDAY
"Rejoice, Beloved Christians"

The minister told the sexton to put up this title for his next Sunday's sermon: ARE MINISTERS CRACKED UP? The sexton looked puzzled, but did what he was told. He put up the letters to read OUR MINISTER'S CRACKING UP.

Church Supper Special

Chicken	$3
Beef	$4
Children	$2

Come and work for the Lord.

The pay is not very good.

But the retirement plan is out of this world.

Bulletins

An offering will be taken today for the Convalescent Home for the sick and tired of the Presbyterian church.

A cookbook is being compiled by the ladies of the church. Please submit your favorite recipe, also a short antidote for it.

The senior pastor will be away for two weeks. The staff members during his absence you will find pinned to the church notice board.

Visitors are asked to sing their names at the church entrance.

The heading over a list of subjects of courses to be offered at a Wednesday-evening Bible school read, "Add a little class to your nightlife."

Our young people are preparing the pizza dinner. It will be held in perish hall.

Cars

A youth group, hoping for donations to help with summer camp expenses, scheduled a day of service for members of the congregation who wanted odd jobs done around their homes. A rich elder said to a teenage boy, "I have two gallons of orange paint. If you paint the porch out back, I'll see that the youth group gets a good donation."

Two hours later the youth came to the door, "Well, I finished the job. But, sir, that's no Porsche. It's a Ferrari!"

Passing through a small town a deacon noticed a sign at a gas station: LAST CHANCE TO BUY $1.05 PER GALLON GAS. STATE LINE 15 MILES.

He had his tank filled, then asked, "How much is gas across the line?"

Replied the attendant, "Ninety-five cents."

A well-to-do youth sponsor, out for a ride in his new luxury car, had an accident. Though he escaped unhurt, his car was wrapped around a tree trunk. Said one of his young people, "See—his Mercedes bends!"

A minister posted a sign at his reserved parking space in the church lot: OLD PROVERB: HE WHO PARKS IN MINISTER'S SPACE MUST PREACH SUNDAY SERMON.

POLICEMAN (*approaching first-time visitor to church after the service):* Why did you park in that area marked NO PARKING?

VISITOR: Because the sign said: FINE FOR PARKING.

A certain type of miracle occurs in parking lots all over the USA. A car pulls into a space marked for the handicapped. Then a person emerges from the car completely healed.

The best device for clearing a driveway of snow is a kid who wants to use the car.

Sign in lot: CHURCH PARKING ONLY. WE WILL NOT FORGIVE THOSE WHO TRESPASS AGAINST US.

Cemeteries

When a stranger was buried in a church graveyard, the members were so distressed that they put up this notice: THIS GRAVEYARD IS EXCLUSIVELY RESERVED FOR THE DEAD WHO ARE LIVING IN THIS PARISH.

This announcement appeared in a local church bulletin in England. "The maintenance of the church graveyard is becoming increasingly costly. It would be a great help if parishioners would do their best to tend their own graves."

Children

A small lad was discussing with one of his buddies the minister's sermon which had been on the story of the sheep and the goats. Lamented the lad, "Me, I don't know which I am. Mother calls me her 'lamb,' and Father calls me 'kid.'"

The sign read: FOR RENT—NO CHILDREN. Answering the bell, the landlady saw a smiling nine-year-old standing there.

"Ma'am, I see your apartment is for rent, and I don't have any children—just me and my parents."

Behind the engaging lad stood a hopeful young couple. They got the apartment.

An evangelist was dining at the home of a church member. Their little boy, who had been watching the guest's every move, blurted out, "Let me see you eat like a horse."

The surprised evangelist said, "What do you mean?"

The boy replied, "My mother said that every time you come here you eat like a horse."

An eleven-year-old boy's prayer: "Dear God: My mom says I can stay out after school only till it gets dark. Please make the sun stand still. I figured if you did it once, you could probably do it again."

A tiny four-year-old, spending a night away from home, knelt at her hostess's knee to say her prayers. Expecting the usual promptings, but getting none, she prayed thus, "Please God, 'scuse me because I can't remember my prayers, and I'm staying with a lady who doesn't know any."

The mother apologized to her unexpected ministerial guest for serving the apple pie without cheese. Her son slipped quietly away from the table for a moment, then returned with a small piece of cheese, which he laid on the guest's plate.

The visitor smiled thankfully at the lad, and putting the cheese in his mouth, remarked, "You must have sharper eyes than your mother, sonny. Where did you find it?"

The boy replied with a flush of pride, "In the mouse-trap."

A little boy, deciding to run away from home, kept running around the block. When a policeman asked what he was doing, he said he was running away from home.

"But you can't be," replied the officer, "because you're just running around the block."

The boy explained, "My mother told me not to cross the street."

Little girl's definition of conscience: "Something that makes you tell your mother before your brother or sister does."

Asked by his grandfather how he liked his first day at Daily Vacation Bible School, a little boy said, "It's just great. We go outside to play, and when we come back in, God has the juice and cookies all ready for us."

Children in Church

During the sermon a father became annoyed with the misbehavior of his five-year-old son, who was also getting disapproving stares from nearby worshipers. Suddenly the exasperated father picked up his son and started down the aisle. Looking back over his father's shoulder, the little fellow interrupted the sermon by calling out a plea to the congregation, "Please pray for me!"

When an infant was presented by its parents for dedication in the morning service, a little girl in church for the first time asked what was happening. Her father said, "His parents are giving the baby to God."

Seeing the minister return the baby to its parents, the youngster commented, "Guess God didn't want *that* one."

A seven-year-old girl, who attended church with her grandmother regularly, remarked that when she grew up she wanted to marry a man just like "our pastor," but added, "but I'm not going to let him be a pastor."

When grandma asked why not, the little lass replied, "Well, if he had to preach, he couldn't ever sit by me in church."

A church was having a prayer of dedication for its new stained-glass windows. Glancing at the scenes in those windows, a little lad exclaimed, "Oh, goody! Cartoons for Sunday morning!"

Returning to his seat in a crowded church, a small boy asked a lady on the end of a row, "Did I step on your feet when I went out?"

"Well," smiled the woman, ready to accept the boy's apology, "as a matter of fact, you did."

"Good," exclaimed the boy, "I must be in the right row then."

A little boy asked his father what was the highest number he had ever counted. Replying that he didn't know, the father asked his son his highest number. It was 973.

"Why did you stop there?"

"Because church was over."

Children in Sunday School

"I want you to be so still that you can hear a pin drop," said a Sunday school teacher, smiling sweetly. After a silence that seemed interminable to the children, a small boy in the corner shouted, "Okay! Let her drop."

A little boy home from Sunday school showed his parents a painting he had done, based on the lesson—the crossing of the Red Sea by the Israelites, chased by the Egyptians.

Surprised to see only a huge blotch of red, the parents asked for an explanation.

Pointing to the blotch of red, he said, "That's the Red Sea."

"Where are the Egyptians?" asked the parents.

"They were all drowned."

"And the Israelites?"

"They've all crossed over."

TEACHER: Why did the Pilgrims come to America?
PUPIL: So they could worship their own way and make other people do the same.

The teacher asked her class of three-year-olds, "Do any of you remember who Matthew was?" No response. "Surely some of you remember who Peter was." A tiny voice from the back squeaked, "I fink he was a wabbit."

TEACHER: Lot was warned to take his wife and flee out of the city. Sadly, she looked back and was turned into a pillar of salt.
LITTLE GIRL: What happened to the flea?

After a discussion on the commandment, "Honor thy father and thy mother," a Sunday school teacher asked her class if there was any commandment that taught brothers and sisters how to treat each other.
A lad from a large family piped up, "Thou shalt not kill."

The Sunday before Thanksgiving a teacher told her Sunday school class, "Let's all think of something to be thankful for."
One girl quickly exclaimed, "That I'm not a turkey."

Christmas

A cartoon showed a seedy-looking beggar on a busy corner in early January, in one hand a hat held out for alms, and in the other a placard which read: TO GIVE AFTER CHRISTMAS—THAT IS TRUE COMPASSION.

When a child in a suburban Philadelphia Sunday school was asked where Jesus was born, he answered, "Philadelphia."

The teacher said, "No, try again."

The child said, "Pittsburgh."

When the teacher again indicated a wrong answer, the child asked, "Where was it, then?"

"Bethlehem," replied the teacher.

"Oh," retorted the child, "I knew it was somewhere in Pennsylvania."

A five-year-old had one line in a Christmas pageant. Appearing in angel's garb, he was to say, "Behold, I bring you good tidings!" After practice the lad asked his mother what "tidings" meant. She explained that it meant news.

At the performance, momentarily forgetting his line, he recovered in time to shout out, "Boy, do I got news for you!"

A mother, concerned over her little son's potential behavior when some Christmas company was scheduled, asked, "Jeremy, are you going to be good when Joe and Mary come over later?"

Little Jeremy asked, "Are Jesus' parents coming *here?*"

After the family sang some carols, four-year-old Johnny commented, "Wasn't it good of the shepherds to put on clean clothes when they went to see baby Jesus?"

Mother asked, "What do you mean?"

Johnny explained, "We just sang, 'While Shepherds Washed Their Socks by Night.'"

One Christmas season the front doors of a church were decorated to resemble a brightly wrapped holiday gift. A sign read: PLEASE OPEN BEFORE CHRISTMAS.

Three-year-old Paul loved to sing Christmas carols. Home from Sunday school he asked his parents to sing "Silent Night" over and over. Puzzled, they listened intently as he sang, "Silent night, holy night, Paul is calm, Paul is bright."

A little girl was asked what she was going to give her brother for Christmas. "I don't know," she answered.
"What did you give him last year?"
"The chicken pox."

Christmas is when people want their pasts forgotten, and their presents remembered.

Church

A group touring Westminster Abbey in London heard the guide list the famous people buried within its walls. During a momentary silence a little old lady's voice blurted out loud and clear, "Anybody been saved here lately?"

While an associate pastor made the announcements in the middle of the Sunday morning service, the pastor left the platform to go downstairs to give an object lesson in junior church. A newcomer whispered to the friend who had invited him, "That's the first minister I ever saw take a coffee break during the service."

MEMBER OF FIRST CHURCH: My church is like a machine I once read about. It had hundreds of wheels, cogs, pulleys, belts, gears, and lights, all of which moved or lit up at the touch of a button.

MEMBER OF SECOND CHURCH: What did it do?

MEMBER OF FIRST CHURCH: Oh, it didn't do anything—but it did run beautifully.

A newcomer asked, "Why do you always sing 'Amen' at the end of your songs?"

The usher replied, "I suppose it's because we sing hymns."

A visitor asked a minister how many members he had in his church. When the minister answered, "Eighty," the visitor asked how many were active.

"Eighty," replied the minister.

"My," remarked the visitor, "you must have an unusual church to have 100 percent active membership."

"Well," admitted the minister, "forty are active for me, and forty are active against me."

Definition of church aisle: bridal path.

The lights went out in the evening service. The pastor asked people to raise their hands. Then he said, "Many hands make light work."

A little boy was taken by his parents to a new church which had long services, both morning and evening. On his third Sunday the boy noticed on the annex wall a list of the names of those who had lost their lives in World War II. The father explained, "They are the names of the men and women who died in the service."

The boy asked, "Which one, morning or evening?"

Church Attendance

Sadly the pastor told his board, "Brethren, I feel we should drop our midweek prayer meeting."

This caused a furor among the board members, who indignantly insisted that the prayer meeting had value and must continue by all means.

"But, my brethren," said the pastor, "what you don't seem to know is that we haven't had our midweek prayer meeting for six months."

MOTHER: Son, get out of bed, and go to church.

SON: I don't want to go.

MOTHER: Get up and go.

SON: They don't like me there any more. I don't want to go.

MOTHER (*20 minutes later*): Son, get up and go to church.

SON: Give me two good reasons why I should go.

MOTHER: All right. You're forty-two years old, and you're the pastor.

A church in California's San Fernando Valley stopped buying from its regular office supplier. Reason was that when they ordered some small pencils to be used in the pew for visitors to register, the dealer sent golf pencils, each stamped with the words: PLAY GOLF NEXT SUNDAY.

FIRST PASTOR: Absence makes the heart grow fonder.

SECOND PASTOR: How some people must love the church.

Awesome is when the pastor enters the sanctuary, glances at the small Sunday-night crowd, then realizes it is actually Sunday morning.

Committees

A new pastor, surveying his big lawn as the grass began to grow in the spring, asked his parsonage committee, "Who cuts the lawn?"

Immediately and decisively came the chairman's answer, "The former pastor, Reverend Johnson, used to do it."

The new pastor quickly replied, "I just phoned the Reverend Johnson in his new pastorate, and he won't do it."

An African in the USA for seminary training went to his first American football game. He noticed that both teams went into a huddle before every play.

"What do you think of this sport?" asked a friend.

"Not a bad sport," he replied, "but they have too many committee meetings."

In the midst of a stormy board session one member shouted at another, "You are the most unreasonable, insensitive man I've ever met."

"Order, order!" yelled the chairman, "you seem to forget that I'm in the room."

A winning vote is like a face: the ayes are above the noes.

CHAIRMAN: It seems unanimous that we cannot agree.

BOARD MEMBER: The chairman of this committee annoys me.

SECOND MEMBER: Why?

FIRST MEMBER: Because he always keeps right on talking when I'm interrupting him.

A bulletin noted that committee chairmen were looking for members to serve on standing committees or task farces.

The ideal committee is composed of three members with one sick, and another absent.

Communism

In a Communist country a guest speaker was lecturing on the increasing prosperity of the Soviet people. In the back row Sokolsky raised his hand, "Comrade lecturer, what you say is interesting, but where has all the meat gone?"

Next day the same lecturer gave another talk on the growing standard of living in the Soviet Union. In the back row Ravinoff raised his hand, "I don't want to know what happened to the meat, but can you tell me what happened to Sokolsky?"

Two Russian students were held up on the streets of New York City. Handing over their wallets to the gunmen, they said something to each other in their own language.

"You guys foreigners?" the gunmen asked.

"We are from Russia," said one of the students.

The gunmen talked together for a moment, then handed the wallets back. "Here, we wouldn't want you guys to get the wrong impression of America."

Courtship

The story of many a romance: he came, he saw, he concurred.

"Young man," said the angry father, "didn't you hear the clock strike four when you brought my daughter home this morning?"

"Yes, sir," replied the lad. "It was going to strike eleven, but I grabbed the gongs and held them so it wouldn't disturb you."

The father turned away, muttering, "Why didn't I think of that in my day?"

"Will you love me when I'm gray?" asked the young girl of her steady.

"Yes, I'm sure I will," he said. "I've loved six shades already."

GIRL: Why aren't you married?
SEMINARY STUDENT: I'm looking for the perfect girl.
GIRL: Have you found her yet?
SEMINARY STUDENT: Yes, but she was looking for the perfect man.

WANT AD: "Farmer wants to marry woman, 35, with tractor. Send picture of tractor."

Criticism

A British columnist, commenting on the censorious attitude of two music critics, remarked, "Had they been present at the feeding of the five thousand, one would have complained that there was no lemon to go with the fish, and the other would have lamented the absence of butter for the loaves."

Most people don't object to criticism if it's favorable.

A first-year seminary student, sitting down in church one Sunday morning and noticing that the guest preacher was one of his professors known for his dullness, muttered out, "Oh, no!"

Sitting beside a lady he didn't know, he felt he should explain. "That's Mr. Dry up there. He's my professor at seminary. I had him three days this week, and now this'll be the fourth time. He's so dry!"

A smile came across her face. She asked, "Do you know who I am?"

"No."

"I am Mrs. Dry, wife of your professor."

The student asked, "Do you know who I am."

She replied, "No"

He exclaimed, "Praise the Lord!"

The person who growls all day will feel dog-tired at night.

Critics are people who are quick on the flaw.

Denominations

A Baptist took a Presbyterian friend to a church business meeting which became rather hectic and heated. After the meeting, the Baptist remarked, "Our congregational form of government is heavenly."

Commented the Presbyterian, "I think so too. That's the only place it will work."

Someone said to Billy Graham, "Are you among that narrow group that believes that only Baptists will be saved?

Graham replied, "I'm even more narrow than that. I believe half the Baptists won't be saved."

A trucker wanted to drive a huge trailer out of New York City when traffic would be lightest. A policeman advised him that 8:30 Sunday mornings Catholics would be at mass, Protestants sleeping since their services were later, and Jews out of town after their Sabbath.

So the trucker left Sunday at 8:30 A.M. As he drove out of the Lincoln Tunnel, he was struck from behind by a Seventh Day Adventist.

Speaking at a Baptist assembly, a church historian said, "Many of you trace your history back to the sixteenth century. Some trace your beginnings to the Day of Pentecost, others to John the Baptist. You're wrong. The origin of the Baptists goes back to the Book of Genesis where Abraham said to Lot, "You go your way, and I'll go mine."

A candidate running for political office traveled to a small town to speak. Anxious to discover the denominational affiliation of the majority of his audience, he began, "My grandfather was a Baptist." Silence.

"But my grandmother belonged to the Presbyterian church." Silence.

"My father and mother were Lutherans." Silence.

"But my aunt attended the Episcopalian church." He was interrupted with loud applause. He continued, "And I have always followed my aunt."

A man waxed eloquent, "My denomination is torn with a fierce dispute. One group says that baptism is 'in the name of the Father,' while the other section insists baptism is 'into the name of the Father.' I belong to one of these parties. I feel strongly about it. I would gladly die for it, but I forget which it is."

Learning that a widowed mother was keeping her three small daughters away from church because they lacked suitable clothes, the Methodist Ladies Circle corrected the condition with a generous supply of beautiful clothes. When still the children did not appear in church, the Methodist ladies inquired about their absence.

The mother sweetly thanked them for the clothes, and explained, "The girls looked so nice that I sent them to the Presbyterian church."

WOMAN: My friends belong to a wide variety of churches.

NEIGHBOR: My bishop would like to see more unity among the denominations. He's interested in the economical movement

---

Rt. Rev. Charles Francis Hall, Episcopal Bishop of New Hampshire, while attending the 1968 Lambeth Conference in London, was to attend a special service at Westminster Abbey. His wife, out shopping with another bishop's wife, realizing it was almost time for the service at the Abbey, jumped into a taxi, directing the driver, "Take us to the cathedral."

He deposited them at the Roman Catholic cathedral. Not realizing where they were, they marched up to an usher, "We're bishops' wives. Where do we sit?"

No one recalls the response of the usher, but the whole story made the front page of London newspapers the next day.

Three men were discussing what they would be, if not what they were, denominationally.

The Catholic said, "I'd be an Episcopalian."

The Methodist said, "I'd be a Baptist."

The Lutheran said, "I'd be ashamed of myself."

A group was discussing which church the Lord would join if he were here on earth today. An Episcopalian suggested that, since his denomination could trace its ministers back to the apostles, he would probably join their church.

A Presbyterian replied that the Lord would join his church because he was one of the original elders.

A Baptist spoke up, "Let me ask a question before I answer. Why did he leave the Baptist church in the first place?"

A woman, asked her church affiliation, replied, "I'm a Lutheran, but my husband is nondimensional."

A member of the Plymouth Brethren lost his leg in an accident. Rushed to a Congregational hospital, he was operated on by an Episcopalian surgeon, and cared for by a Presbyterian nurse. He then advertised for a wooden leg in a Disciples' paper. A Methodist widow, whose handicapped husband had been a Baptist, took his artificial leg out of storage, and sent it by a Lutheran delivery man to this needy believer. When the amputee learned the full story, he sighed, "I guess I'm a United Brethren."

A little boy whose parents never went to church, asked what church he attended, replied, " I'm a seven-day absentist."

Two churches in a little town, one Presbyterian and the other Christian, decided to form one church. When the idea was broached to the presiding elder in the Presbyterian church, he replied, "I've been a Presbyterian for sixty years. I couldn't become a Christian now."

A Baptist, entering a Congregational church, prayed, "Lord, if there's a spark here, water it."

An ad in a Hong Kong newspaper: "Teeth extracted by the latest Methodists."

Devil

At an ordination examination a young candidate declared he did not believe in a personal devil. Embarrassingly shifting in their seats, the ministers were about to vote against ordaining him, although he had given perfectly orthodox answers in all other areas of doctrine.

Then the oldest pastor present made this comment, "Brethren, I see no reason for refusing this young man simply because now he does not believe in a personal devil. This matter will take care of itself. He won't be a pastor of a church two weeks before he changes his mind."

During the building of a new Episcopalian cathedral in Denver a fault was discovered in the footings that required tearing down the incomplete west front and redoing it. The monsignor of the Immaculate Conception Cathedral, a few blocks away, chided his friend, Dean Bell of St. John's, "There is something wrong with Anglican foundations, I hear."

A short time later, during an electrical storm, lightning struck and destroyed a spire at Immaculate Conception. Dean Bell hurried to the monsignor and said, "Whereas my enemies are from below, yours are from above."

When an open-air preacher mentioned the devil, a heckler called out, "Don't you know the devil is dead?"

The preacher shot back, "You poor orphan."

An indignant parishioner phoned her minister, "I tried to get you yesterday, but I couldn't reach you."

"Monday is my day off," said the minister.

"The devil never takes a day off," she said.

"Since when," retorted the minister, "is the devil my example?"

Dinners

CHURCH BULLETIN: The Ladies Society will be selling their new cookbook at the church supper this Wednesday night. The proceeds will help purchase a stomach pump for our community hospital.

A father, taking his family to dinner after Sunday morning service, warned his little boy not to take any of the free candies by the cash register. While paying the bill, he noticed a small hand slowly slide toward the bowl of candies. After giving it a hard slap, he turned to find it was the hand of a petite, elderly lady.

DELEGATE *(Attending a denominational convention and ordering breakfast the second morning)*: I'll have two cold eggs, undercooked hash browns, a stale Danish, and very weak coffee.

WAITRESS: Oh, I can't serve you that, sir.

DELEGATE: Why not? You did it yesterday morning.

Overheard at dinnertime during church convention: "This restaurant's 'catch of the day' is obviously your waiter's eye."

Education (Children in College)

To CHRISTIAN COLLEGE PRESIDENT: How many students do you have in your school?

PRESIDENT: One in ten.

A mother reminded her son at the airport, as he left for the new semester, to write often.

Another mother, overhearing the request, quietly gave this advice, "The surest way to get your son to write home is to send him a letter saying 'Here's one hundred dollars. Spend it any way you wish.'"

"And that will make my son write me?"

"Yes, indeed, if you forget to enclose the money."

A father received a letter from his son at college. "Dear Dad: I mi$$ you. Gue$$ what I need mo$t? Plea$e $end $ome $oon. Love, your $on, Jame$."

The father answered, "Dear James: We knOw yOu lOve cOllege. We spOke abOut this at nOOn. Write anOther letter sOOn. GOOd bye, nOw, SOn. LOve, yOur dad."

Education (Curriculum)

Graffiti on the wall of a Purdue University building:
IF GOD HAD WANTED US TO USE THE METRIC SYSTEM, HE WOULD HAVE CHOSEN TEN DISCIPLES.

Graffiti on a blackboard at Dallas Seminary:
DISPENSATIONALISM IS NOT FOR THIS AGE.

Education (Degrees)

A visitor at Princeton University's graduation ceremonies some years ago noted that a number of honorary degree recipients were men of wealth who had the reputation of contributing to the nation's colleges.

The visitor asked the president, "Do you bestow these honors to loosen their purse strings?"

"I wouldn't say it so bluntly," replied the president, "but we do seem to get richer by degrees."

A pastor who bought a doctor's degree from a diploma mill defended his action by quoting part of 1 Timothy 3:13: "They that have used the office of a deacon well purchase to themselves a good degree."

Education (Library)

The coed asked for a good theological book to read. The obliging librarian asked, "Do you want something light, or do you prefer the heavier books?"

"Really doesn't matter," the coed assured her. "I have my car outside."

STUDENT: Why is the librarian at our Bible college suspicious of the accounting office?

SECOND STUDENT: Because the people who work there are bookkeepers.

Education (Prayer in School)

FIRST TEACHER: Do you think we'll ever get prayer back in the public schools?

SECOND TEACHER: As long as there are final exams, there'll always be prayer in the public schools.

A teacher reported to the principal that she had seen a group of children kneeling in a corner of the playground during the noon break. Calling the children to the office, the principal asked for an explanation.

"We were playing poker," they replied.

"Oh, I'm so relieved," sighed the principal. "I thought you were praying."

Education (Professors)

A Salvation Army lass was passing out tracts in a crowded bus. Approaching a dignified-looking man, she said, "Sir, I hope you're a Christian."

The man of dignity replied, "Why, I am a theological professor."

Confused by his reply, the lass put a hand on his arm, "My good man, don't let that stand in your way."

A near-sighted professor, an expert in insects, had his office walls covered with framed bugs. His students, attempting a practical joke, took the body of one bug, the legs of another, and the head of yet another, and glued them all together. "What kind of bug is this?" the students asked, as they brought him the specimen.

Eyeing the bug closely, the professor replied, "Students, this is a humbug."

A professor said to his class, "If there are any dumb-bells in this class, please stand up."

After a short wait a tall youth in the back of the room rose to his feet.

"So you consider yourself a dumbbell?" the professor asked.

"No, sir," replied the youth. "I just hated to see you standing there all alone."

A Greek professor took his torn trousers to a tailor with a Greek name. The tailor looked at the slacks and asked, "Euripedes?"

"Yes," replied the professor, "Eumenides?"

Education (Results)

A recent graduate of a well-known self-improvement course exclaimed enthusiastically, "I'll never forget peoples' names since I took that Sam Carnegie course."

A high-school senior on an application to college wrote, "I want to be a psychologist. I plan on taking as many psychology courses as possible and may some day turn out to be another Fraud."

Mother to little girl getting off the bus after her first day of school: "What did you learn today?"
Little girl: "Nothing, I guess. The teacher said I have to come back tomorrow."

Transferred to a Christian day school, a little girl brought home a batch of test papers. "Mother, I made one hundred today!"
Her elated mother said, "Tell me about it."
The girl replied, "I made fifty in arithmetic, thirty in spelling, and twenty in geography.

"A question on a course in U.S. History asked, "What are the last two lines of the first verse of 'The Star Spangled Banner'?"
One answer read, "Play ball."

A young man, new on the job, was told to sweep out the store.
Surprised, the new employee protested, "But I'm a college graduate."
The manager quietly replied, "Well, that's all right, I'll show you how."

A college student, who enrolled for a summer-school class, goofed off the entire six weeks. When he didn't pass, he complained, "I really don't think I deserve an F"

"Neither do I," came the professor's reply, "but unfortunately it's the lowest grade I'm authorized to give."

Education (Romance)

At a Bible college chapel service the Dean of Men made this announcement: "There's too much romance going on here. The Dean of Women and I are determined to stop kissing on the campus."

Flustered at the roar of laughter that greeted his remark, the Dean of Men continued, "What I mean is—there's too much kissing going on under our noses."

Excuses

A traffic cop flagged down a young driver, glancing at his license, then remarked, "Oh, so you're a preacher. Now don't go telling me you didn't see that stop sign."

Replied the youthful minister, "Oh, to be sure I saw the sign, officer. The point is—I didn't see you."

A boss said to his new young accountant, "Do you believe in life after death?"

When the puzzled accountant said that he did, the boss seemed relieved. "You see—about a half-hour after you left to attend your grandfather's funeral yesterday afternoon, he came in here to see you!"

A teacher received this note, "Please excuse my son Billy's absence on Thursday as it was Ash Wednesday. (Signed) My MOTHER."

Two Sunday morning golfers were playing poorly. One said, "I should have stayed home and gone to church."

To which the other replied, "I couldn't have gone to church anyway. My wife is sick in bed."

Why are fire trucks red?

A pastor gave this explanation. "Fire trucks have four wheels and eight men. Four and eight are twelve. Twelve inches make a foot, and a ruler is a foot. The ruler of the Finns declared war on the Russians. The Russians are red. Fire trucks are always rushin'. Therefore, fire trucks are always red.

"If you think this reasoning is wild, then you ought to hear some explanations people give for not coming to church."

The new preacher looked sternly at Deacon Smith. "I heard you went to a ball game instead of church last Sunday."

"That's a lie," said the deacon indignantly. "And I've got the fish to prove it!"

An excuse is the skin of a reason stuffed with a lie.

Family

A lady, newly converted, told a visiting evangelist that God was calling her to preach.

He asked if she had any children.

"Oh, yes," she replied. "I have a large family. All my children are still at home."

The evangelist's face lit up. "Glory be! God has not only called you to preach, but he's given you a congregation as well."

A father and mother told their seven-year-old they had to move to a larger house because another baby was coming.

"Aw, that won't work," frowned the youngster. "He'll just follow us."

BOY TO PAL: When company stays too long at your house, how do you get rid of them?

PAL: We just treat them like members of the family.

An eight-year-old, back home after attending church with a friend, told about the service. "The preacher asked everyone who had family commotions at their house to raise their hand. So I did."

Arriving for a visit, the lady asked her small granddaughter, "Joanie, how do you like your new baby brother?"

"Oh, he's all right," the child struggled. "But there were a lot of other things we needed worse."

Fathers and Daughters

A minister, speaking at a college chapel, was introduced as the father of seven daughters. He began by telling them, "I feel right at home on a college campus because I live in a girl's dormitory. I am the Dean of Women. And if ever a little son comes along after these seven daughters, we have a name already picked out for him: 'Henry the 8th.'"

On other occasions when a presiding officer would mention his seven daughters in his introduction, the minister would simply say, "With so many women around the house, I was always happy for even a **MAIL**box out front."

A little girl asked her father why it rained when there were so many clouds in the sky. The father answered, "I don't know."

The little girl asked her father three more questions to which he gave the same answer, "I don't know."

After a pause she asked, "Daddy, do you mind if I ask you questions?"

"Of course not," the father replied. "How would you learn if you didn't ask them?"

Father to daughter's fiancé who was always jumping from one job to another. "My daughter says you have that certain something. I only wish you had something certain."

Fathers and Sons

The sixth-grader walked unhesitatingly up to his father and said, "Dad, here's my report card. And here also is an old one of yours I found in the attic."

A father had been trying to stimulate his son to greater effort in his schoolwork. "My boy," he said, preparing to deliver his master stroke, "do you know what Abraham Lincoln was doing when he was your age?"

"No, sir," admitted the lad. "But I know what he was doing when he was *your* age."

SON: That math problem you helped me with last night was all wrong, Dad.
FATHER: All wrong, was it? Well, I'm sorry.
SON: Don't worry about it. None of the other fathers got it right either.

A little boy climbed into the barber's chair. "I want my hair cut just like daddy's. With a hole in the top."

A department-store Santa Claus asked a little boy if he had anything to say. Came his reply, "My daddy says to use your head this year and not bring anything he has to assemble."

Wanting to take his wife out for the evening, a father dropped his ten-year-old son off at grandpa's house. As the father went out the door, grandpa asked, "When do you want him back?"

"When he's nineteen!" reported the father.

A father, gloomily studying his son's report card, sighed, "Well, one thing is definitely in your favor. With these grades you couldn't possibly be cheating."

The story is told of an introspective five-year-old boy who took an interest in how babies came to be. The father explained how the mother's body protected the baby and how the circulation of her blood kept it warm and provided nourishment.

At dinner a few evenings later, the boy said, "Daddy, you should know that I really don't have to pay any attention to you. Mother is my blood relative, but you're not. You are only related to me by marriage!"

A little boy looked up at his daddy, and asked, "Before you married mom, who told you how to drive?"

A father asked his son, a junior in college, if he were in the top half of his class.

The son replied, "I'm one of those who make the top half possible."

Friends

Friends are those rare people who ask how we are, and then wait to hear the answer.

Golf

Sitting down for breakfast on a lovely spring Saturday morning, a wife said to her husband, "I know how much you'd like to play golf today. But I need you for chores around the house. Please, not one word about golf."

Her husband reassured her, "Don't worry, I won't mention it. Please pass the putter."

A church elder stepped to the first tee, took a mighty swing, and made a hole in one.

"How wonderful," said his pastor and playing partner. "Now I'll take my practice swing, and then we can start to play."

A pastor was having a bad morning on the golf course. "I'd move heaven and earth just to break ninety today," he exclaimed.

"You'd better concentrate on heaven," his friend replied. "You've already moved about a ton of earth."

WIFE: You think so much of your golf game that you don't even remember when we were married.
HUSBAND: Sure I do. It was the day I sank the forty-foot putt.

Nothing increases your golf score like witnesses.

Gossip

When a gossip approached a wise, old deacon with "What's going on?" the deacon replied, "I am!"

The trouble with stretching the truth is that it's apt to snap back.

Gossip is changing an earful into a mouthful.

A small town is where it's no sooner done than said.

Gossip is something negative that is developed and then enlarged.

A gossip is someone who can give you all the details without knowing any of the facts.

She joined a sewing cir-cle—and now she's needling everyone.

Her gossip is strictly her-say.

He burns his scandals at both ends.

He's an expert on hintimation.

Government

One commentator warned adults that when telling a small child that Washington never told a lie, to be sure to make it very clear that they are referring to the man and not to the city.

Amid a mixture of amens and chuckles, a member of the Arizona House of Representatives offered this prayer to open a morning session: "Lord, make all of our words gracious and tender today, for tomorrow we may have to eat them."

A little girl, whose family always had prayer together every evening, took her turn the night after her father had been elected to Congress. She prayed, "Good bye, Lord; we're going to Washington."

A Navajo Indian sent the following message to Congress: "Be careful with your immigration laws. We weren't with ours."

A middle-aged couple on vacation decided to spend a night at Watergate Hotel in Washington. Sitting around in their room, the wife said, "I'm a little leery. This place could be bugged."

Her husband replied, "Oh, it's sixteen years since the big episode. It's perfectly safe."

Nevertheless she insisted that he do a little investigation. Sure enough, he discovered a lump in the carpet under the bed. So he got hold of a screwdriver and unfastened the little gadget.

Next morning the front office phoned to ask if they spent a good night. They assured the woman at the desk that it had been a most pleasant night. Then the woman on the phone mentioned that the room below theirs had just reported that a chandelier had fallen on their floor.

A U.S. Navy ship was coming up a foggy channel in Puget Sound. Noting a blip on radar that indicated some object in its path, the captain radioed, "Take evasive action. We are on a dead-collision course."

A few seconds later came the answer, "You take evasive action."

Getting on the phone, the captain said, "This is an admiral speaking. Take evasive action."

Seconds later came the reply, "This is a radio operator second-class."

The captain firmly responded, "This is a U.S. Navy ship."

After a brief period of silence came the radio operator's voice again. "This is the United States Coast Guard Lighthouse!"

> Fairy tales used to begin, "Once upon a time . . ."
> Now they start, "When I am elected . . ."

Grandchildren

> TEACHER *(pointing to her chest):* This is where your heart is.
>
> PUPIL *(from back row):* Mine is where I sit down.
>
> TEACHER: Whatever gives you that idea?
>
> PUPIL: Because every time I do something good, my grandma pats me there and says, "Bless your little heart."

> On a visit to his grandparents little Bobby was taken to an expensive restaurant as a special treat. They were surprised when the nine-year-old ordered a hamburger.
>
> "In a place like this," his grandfather said, smiling, "why don't you try something different, something you've never had?"
>
> "That's what I'm doing," announced Bobby. "I've sure never had a ten dollar hamburger before!"

> Grandchildren are a double blessing. They're a blessing when they come, and they're a blessing when they go.

Gratitude

> At a banquet in New York City at which pork was the main dish, Daddy Hall, an Episcopalian rector and open-air preacher known for his homespun, down-to-earth phraseology, prayed this blessing, "Dear Lord, if thou canst bless under grace what you cursed under law, then bless this bunch while they munch this lunch."

Because at a banquet no clergymen were present to ask the blessing, a well-known actor was conscripted to say the grace. He began, "There being no clergymen present, let us give thanks."

Dr. Alexander Whyte of Edinburgh, Scotland, was famous for his pulpit prayers which always included words of thanksgiving. One stormy morning a member thought to himself, "The preacher will have nothing to thank God for on a wretched morning like this."

But Dr. Whyte began his prayer, "We thank thee that it is not always like this."

Preachers always enjoy the Thanksgiving service because that's when they can talk turkey to their congregation.

Hardship

Hardship is when we have to do without things our grandparents never heard of.

People who do not believe in prayer make an exception when tragedy strikes.

A new convert gave this testimony: "I have a mountain-top experience every day. One day I'm on top of the mountain. Then the next day the mountain is on top of me."

An almost-deaf old gentleman decided that buying a hearing aid was much too expensive. Instead, he wrapped an ordinary piece of wire around one ear.

"How can that wire help you hear better?" a friend asked.

"Now," he replied, "everybody talks louder."

The man who can smile when something has gone wrong may have just thought of someone he can blame it on.

A fellow was up to his ears in debt. His car wouldn't run. His mother-in-law moved in. He lost his job. And when he phoned Dial-a-Prayer, he was put on hold.

A window in a New York City jewelry store contained a display of all types of crosses. Underneath stood a sign that read: EASY TERMS.

Humility (and Pride)

When a down-hearted minister knelt at the altar, repeating, "I am nothing, nothing," his assistant was overcome by this show of humility and joined him. The janitor saw them, and moved by it all, did the same. Whereupon the assistant whispered to the minister, "Now, look *who* thinks he's nothing."

A man wrote a book *Humility and How I Attained It,* and suggested to the publisher that the book include eight large-size photos of the author.

A preacher said to his congregation, "I intended to speak on the theme of humility, but the crowd isn't nearly big enough. Therefore, I'm going to change my topic."

A man, after receiving a compliment, remarked, "I bet you tell the same thing to everyone who's brilliant."

A man had earned perfect attendance pins each year for so many years that, hanging from his shoulder, the string of medals reached all the way to the floor. But he missed one Sunday for the first time because he broke his leg when he tripped over his string of medals.

A pompous air force officer, newly promoted, sat in his new office. When a workman with kit in hand walked into his office, to impress the visitor the officer picked up the phone, and said, "Yes, General, I'll call President Reagan this afternoon. I won't forget. I understand that the president wants to talk to me." Then hanging up, the officer asked the young workman, "And what may I do for you?"

"Oh," replied the workman, "I just came to connect your phone."

A cartoon in *The Anglican Digest* pictured a rector standing outside his study door, contemplating his name plate on which his name was followed by four impressive doctor's degrees, which in turn was followed by the words in large print: AND YOUR HUMBLE SERVANT.

One of life's major temptations is the impulse to leave the price tag on an expensive gift you are giving someone.

You might as well laugh at yourself now and then. Everyone else does.

The bigger a man's head gets, the easier it is to fill his shoes.

Man is the only animal you can pat on the back, and his head swells.

He's always letting off esteem.

Husbands and Wives

A marriage counselor was trying to help a couple who fought a lot. When he heard the wife call her husband, "Hon," the counselor interrupted, "There's still hope for your marriage if you call him 'Hon.'"

"I've been calling him that for several years," the wife retorted, "Attila the Hon."

A timid man said to his wife, "We're not going out tonight—and that's semifinal."

WIFE: Will you love me when I'm old and gray and wrinkled?
HUSBAND: I do.

A woman went to a lawyer about getting a divorce.
LAWYER: Do you have grounds?
CLIENT: Oh, yes, two-and-a-half acres.
LAWYER: Does your husband beat you up?
CLIENT: No, I'm up before him every morning.
LAWYER: Is there infidelity?
CLIENT: No, we have high fidelity.
LAWYER: Then what is the problem?
CLIENT: We've been married two years, and we don't communicate.

A ladies' circle decided to help a family with two sick children who needed frequent blood transfusions. Promptly ten women volunteered to donate blood—their husbands'.

If a husband thinks for one minute that he understands his wife, he has it timed just about right.

A couple celebrated their twenty-fifth wedding anniversary with a dinner date at a plush restaurant. Driving home he sat in the driver's seat. She sat on the other side, almost against the door. She remarked, "Remember how in courtship we used to sit together. We didn't need two seats, did we?"

After a moment's reflection he replied, "*I* haven't moved."

NEWLY MARRIED HUSBAND: I'm beginning to feel like a melon.
BRIDE: Why?
HUSBAND: All I hear is, "Honey, do this," and "Honey, do that."

HUSBAND: Don't forget the Bible says that the husband is the head of the wife.
WIFE: And don't you forget the Bible says that a virtuous woman is a crown to her husband, and the crown is worn on the top of the head.

WIFE: Here's a story about an uneducated man who met a woman and became a scholar in two years.
HUSBAND: That's nothing. I know an intelligent man who met a woman and made a fool of himself in two days.

A farmer and his wife were sleeping in an upstairs bedroom. A tornado hurled them through the air. As they took this unusual trip, his wife cried.

"Why are you crying?" her husband asked.

Replied the wife, "I am so happy!"

"And why are you so happy?" asked the husband.

"Because," the wife responded, "this is the first time we've been out together in twenty-five years."

FIRST WOMAN: Your husband seems to be a man of rare gifts.

SECOND WOMAN: You can say that again! The last one he gave me was fifteen years ago.

Two men were discussing their wives. One said he loved his wife very much, but every time they got into an argument, she became historical.

"You mean 'hysterical,'" the other man replied.

"No, 'historical,'" the man asserted. "She keeps bringing up the past."

WIFE: Whenever I get down in the dumps, I get a new hat.

HUSBAND: I wondered where you got them.

"I've got good news," called the husband as he entered the house at suppertime. "I picked up two tickets for the Bible-school concert on the way home from work."

"Oh, that's wonderful," said the wife. "I'll start dressing right away."

"That's a good idea," he said. "The tickets are for tomorrow night."

WIFE (to disinterested HUSBAND during sermon): Can't you give the pastor a little attention?

HUSBAND: I'm giving him as little attention as I can.

A pastor announced an extra collection at the end of his sermon. He asked "the head of the household" to come forward and deposit the money on the altar. Many husbands rose and came to the front, after getting the money from their wives.

Said a pastor, "I never buy any suits, shirts, or ties unless my wife is there to tell me whether or not I like them."

A pastor, teaching the Young Married Couples class, commented, "Police records indicate that no wife has ever shot her husband while he was drying dishes."

A husband commented, "My wife and I work together in our car. She drives while I steer."

Marriage is an institution held together by two books: checkbook and cookbook.

Hymns

A church bulletin carried this item in the Sunday morning order of worship: "Hymn No. 58—'Gold Will Take Care of You'"

Proofs of a new hymnbook read, "Praised is the Lord by day and praised by night; praised is he when we lie down and praised when we wise up."

A misprint in the hymn titled "Guide Me, O Thou Great Jehovah" made the line: "Land me safe on Canaan's shore" read: "Land my safe on Canaan's shore."

The songleader, aiming at variation, had the women sing the first line, and the men the second.
The women sang, "I may go home someday."
The men followed with "Glad day, glad day."

When a church group was conducting a service in a prison chapel, the leader asked for a favorite hymn.

One of the prisoners, glancing through the hymn-book, called out, "Number Thirty-two."

Looking it up, they discovered the title was "Never Give Up."

A congregation, too poor to buy new hymnals, was offered a sufficient quantity by a pharmaceutical firm in exchange for a bit of advertising. When the hymnals arrived, the church found them lovely looking. Unable to find any hint of advertising on the covers, front or back, inside or outside, or on any of the early pages, they supposed the company had forgotten. But on Christmas Eve when the congregation turned to a well-known carol, they rose to sing:

Hark, the herald angels sing,
Beecham's pills are just the thing,
Peace on earth and mercy mild,
Two for an adult, one for a child.

A songleader, apparently influenced by the yawns of members of the congregation during the singing, introduced the next song by saying, "Please turn over in your hymnbooks. . . ."

Hypocrisy

A wife, looking through her linen closet, exclaimed, "The new maid has stolen two of our towels, the crook!"

"Which towels, dear?" her husband asked.

"You know," she replied, "the ones we got from the hotel in Los Angeles."

A lady came to a stop at the red light. She was directly behind a car filled with young children, driven by their mother, and bearing a big bumper sticker: HONK—IF YOU LOVE JESUS. So the lady in the second car gave a friendly push on the horn, whereupon the mother in the car up front stuck her head out of the window, swore profusely, and yelled, "Can't you see the light's still red?"

A lady tried to sneak her tiny dog through customs. Though knowing she was breaking the law, she also realized how much her pet suffered when away from its mistress. Covering the creature under her fur coat, and smiling her prettiest, she sailed right up to the customs officer at the barrier. All went beautifully—until her coat barked.

Inflation

What keeps millions of people from going into the stock market is the supermarket.

A dollar may not go very far these days—but what it lacks in distance, it makes up in speed.

Inflation: That which causes billionaires to live like they were millionaires.

Inflation has affected the cost of feathers —even down is up.

A church treasurer phoned the local electric company. "I understand there's to be a big increase in rates. Can you tell me what to expect?"

After a pause, the voice on the other end asked, "Are you sitting down?"

The treasurer replied, "No, I'm kneeling."

A preacher pictures a modern Rip Van Winkle going to sleep in 1990 and waking up in 2000. His first thought is to find a pay phone and call his brother to see how his IBM stock, worth thirty thousand dollars when he went to sleep, is doing. To his delight he learns that it is now worth three hundred thousand dollars. Just then the phone operator breaks in to say, "Your three minutes are up. Please deposit one thousand dollars."

The denomination's annual convention had just ended. As a poorly paid preacher, whose expenses had not been subsidized by his church, paid his bill at the very fashionable headquarters hotel, he noticed a sign near the door which read HAVE YOU LEFT ANYTHING?

Walking over to the manager, the preacher suggested, "That sign's wrong. It should read HAVE YOU ANYTHING LEFT?"

In-Laws

"Leaving her husband and her mother home in America, a wife went on a pleasure trip to Europe, including London, Paris, Rome, and Athens. She phoned home from each city, asking how things were.

When she phoned from Athens, she asked, "How's our dog?"

Her husband replied, "He's dead. He climbed out on the roof and fell off."

The wife was terribly disturbed. "You shouldn't have told me so suddenly. You should have told me, when I called from London, that the dog was on the roof. When I called from Paris, that the dog had fallen off the roof. When I called from Rome, that the dog was critical. And then when I called from Athens, that the dog was dead. Please, from now on break bad news to me gently."

Then she asked, "By the way, how's my mother?"

"Oh, she's on the roof," the husband said calmly.

In the midst of a couple's regular quarrel over the character of their families, the wife complained, "You never say anything nice about my family."

"Yes, I do," countered the husband. "I think your mother-in-law is much nicer than mine."

A daughter's nightly prayer: "Dear Lord, I don't ask for anything for myself. Instead, please send my mother a good son-in-law."

An usher was busy escorting wedding guests to their seats. When a finely dressed woman appeared at the back of the church, the usher took her arm and asked, "Are you a friend of the bride?"

"Oh, no," she whispered, "I'm the groom's mother."

The prospective father-in-law asked, "Young man, can you support a family?"

The surprised groom-to-be replied, "Well, no. I was just planning to support your daughter. The rest of you will have to shift for yourselves."

A father said, "Our son and daughter-in-law came up with a foolproof way to save money on food. They bought themselves an economy car—and then began driving it to our house for dinner every night."

If you are a child of God, and you marry a child of the devil, you are surely going to have trouble with your father-in-law.

Interdependence

A man with money and a man with experience joined in a business partnership. Before long, the man with money had the experience, and the man with experience had the money!

Three lifelong friends, on their dream trip of sailing the Pacific in their own yacht, found themselves marooned on a desert island. To their surprise a "genie" appeared on the beach, granting each a wish.

The first said he missed his brokerage business and promptly vanished from the island.

The second said he wished he was playing golf in America, and immediately found himself standing on the first tee of his favorite course.

The third, suddenly feeling very alone, exclaimed, "I wish my friends were back."

A woman in charge of promoting their denominational magazine among the members of her church was given a minute to make an appeal to the congregation. "Please, brothers and sisters, if all of us start our subscription at the same time, and mail it in before the end of the month, then we'll be able to expire together."

An English professor wrote on the board the sentence, "Woman without her man is a savage." Then he asked the students to punctuate it correctly.

The males in the class wrote, "Woman, without her man, is a savage."

The females wrote, "Woman! Without her, man is a savage."

Introductions

Sir Winston Churchill, featured speaker at a banquet, was not introduced till after a long, tedious program, and very late in the evening. He rose, "I have been asked to give a short address, and here it is—Ten Downing Street, and I'm going there right now."

The chairman introduced the three preachers who were scheduled to deliver sermons one after another.

"May the Lord give the first preacher power to provide inspiration here today.

"And may the Lord help the second speaker to convey the seriousness of his message to all assembled here.

"And may the Lord have mercy on the last speaker."

A speaker about to address a college chapel held in a gymnasium, surveying the situation, wondered if there would be a hearing problem. The first row of bleachers was several feet away.

The student who was acting as chairman for chapel that day made his introduction, then whispered, "Speak loud—the agnostics are bad out there."

A guest preacher at a New York City church, who had graduated from Penn State and who was staying at Park Central, was introduced by the pastor as coming from the state pen, and sleeping in Central Park.

A speaker rose to speak after a long, flowery introduction listing his education and achievements, and including several compliments. "You ought to pray for the man who introduced me tonight for he exaggerated so much." Then he added, "And you ought to pray for me for enjoying it so much."

When the scheduled, highly touted preacher had to cancel, the leader explained the situation best he could. Then the substitute tried to smooth things over. "When a window breaks," he began, "you replace it with cardboard, and it does the job."

At the end a man approached, "Don't feel too badly. You're a real pane."

A man who was scheduled to introduce Eleanor Roosevelt asked a friend for help. The friend said, "You don't have to say much. When anyone introduces the president, he simply says, 'Ladies and Gentlemen, the president of the United States.' In fact, the more important the person, the less said the better."

When it came for the introduction, the man introduced her this way, "May I present Eleanor Roosevelt. The less said, the better."

After a long introduction, the speaker began, "That's a lot of gravy for a small potato."

Literature

Home from college at semester break, a girl told her mother that she was going to a movie that evening with other college students. Under questioning she admitted that "the movie had some bad parts, but they won't hurt me."

At that moment the mother was making a tossed salad. With her daughter looking on, she quietly fished out a handful of garbage and dumped it into the salad.

Horrified, the girl exclaimed, "Mother, why did you do that?"

Came the reply, "Since you don't seem to mind filling your mind with garbage, I thought you wouldn't mind filling your stomach too."

NEW FUNERAL DIRECTOR: What magazine do you suggest I read for my occupation?
RETIRING FUNERAL DIRECTOR: *Good Hearsekeeping.*

Lying

A young man, appointed to an important diplomatic government post, was urged to represent his age at twenty-eight, instead of twenty-three, to lend dignity to the choice. The same issue of his local hometown paper that carried the news of his appointment and supposed age also carried a report of his parents' silver wedding anniversary.

A small country church had just concluded a week of revival services and was having a baptismal service in a river on a cold January day. The preacher asked one baptismal candidate, "Is the water cold?"

"Naw!" he replied.

One of the deacons shouted, "Dip him again, preacher. He's lying."

Perjury has been called "truth decay."

Marriage

WIFE *(to marriage counselor):* We haven't agreed on a thing for six years.
HUSBAND: It's seven years.

Marriage involves mathematics for it doubles joys, halves sorrows, and quadruples expenses.

Telegram to newlyweds:
MAY YOU HAVE THE WISDOM OF SOLOMON, THE PATIENCE OF JOB, AND THE CHILDREN OF ISRAEL.

A visitor, asked to say something about his wife and himself at a church couples' club, announced, "My wife and I have been happily married for twelve years. We just celebrated our thirty-seventh wedding anniversary."

A gray-haired couple sat holding hands every Sunday morning during most of the church service. A visitor turned to the wife, "How wonderful that you're still so much in love."

"Love has nothing to do with it," she replied. "I hold Bill's hand to keep him from cracking his knuckles."

Near a large city were two small towns by the names of "Normal" and "Oblong." The wedding page of a church paper carried this headline: NORMAL BOY MARRIES OBLONG GIRL.

The couple stopped dating and started intimidating.

What started out as a diary of their lovers' quarrels turned out to be a big scrapbook.

Their home is often closed for altercations.

Sign over city marriage license bureau: OUT FOR LUNCH. THINK IT OVER.

A bridegroom is a guy who has lost his liberty in the pursuit of happiness.

They get along like two peeves in a pod.

On their thirtieth wedding anniversary the parents received this card from their five children:

To DAD, who for thirty years has ruled the roost, and
To MOM, who for thirty years has ruled the rooster.

Miracles

A public-school teacher was trying to convince a sixth-grader that what he had learned in Sunday school about Moses crossing the Red Sea was nothing out of the ordinary. "Actually," he explained, "Moses and the Israelites simply walked across a three-inch-deep marsh called the Red Sea."

The bright sixth-grader responded, "Wow, then the Lord really did save the day when he drowned the Egyptian army in a puddle of water!"

A man was converted from a life of alcoholism which had caused untold grief to his wife and family. Their house needed painting, their furniture was broken down, and their clothing shabby. His employer, surprised at the change in his life, and learning that he was attending church, said, "Surely, you don't believe all this nonsense about miracles—about turning water into wine and all that."

"Water into wine!" replied the reclaimed alcoholic. "That's nothing! Come up to my house and you'll see whiskey turned into tables, chairs, paint, clothes, and shoes!"

A youngster was telling his family about the lesson he had just had in Sunday school. "It was about Moses crossing the Red Sea. Moses had his engineers build a pontoon bridge across the sea. Then his people crossed it. Then his reconnaissance planes radioed that an Egyptian tank corps was about to cross the bridge. So Moses ordered his jets to blow the bridge up. They did, and Moses and his people were safe."

His father asked, "Are you sure that's how your teacher told the story?"

"Well, not exactly," admitted the boy. "But the way he told it—you wouldn't believe it."

A woman in a doctor's office waiting to have her blood pressure checked waited so long that one of her legs fell asleep. When the nurse finally called her name, she limped into the examining room. Minutes later, when she walked back through the waiting room at her usual brisk pace, two patients who had arrived at the waiting room after her, but had seen her limp into the doctor's examining room, stared in amazement.

One nudged the other, "Didn't I tell you he's the best doctor in town?"

SKEPTIC *(during conversation on Bible stories):* I cannot swallow Jonah.

BELIEVER: You don't have to. God prepared a fish to do that.

Missionaries

MISSIONARY TO CANNIBAL: I understand that you kill people and eat them.

CANNIBAL TO MISSIONARY: I understand that in America you kill people and don't eat them.

A church leader from America was visiting his denomination's missionary field in India. Invited to speak to the national church, the visitor told of headquarter's operations back in the USA. The missionary who was translating sensed that the nationals had no interest in what the American was saying. Ten minutes later, while the visitor was still speaking, some nationals began to come forward. The flustered speaker asked the missionary why people were coming up front.

The missionary replied, "When you started to talk about your headquarter's operations back in America, I began to preach an evangelistic sermon, and I just gave an invitation!"

A favorite story among missionaries concerns ants and the length of missionary service.

In the first year, if the missionaries find ants in the sugar, they throw the sugar out.

In the second year they pick out every ant.

In the third year they pick out some of the a

In the fourth year they say, "Here's the pro

A missionary heard about a convert wh wives.

"You are violating a law of God," said the So you must go and tell four of those wome can no longer live here, or consider you their

The convert thought a few moments, then saia, "I ll wait here. *You* tell them."

After the service the little boy lingered behind and insisted on seeing the missionary.

"Ah, my lad," said the missionary kindly, as he patted the boy's head. "Do you wish to consecrate your life and become a missionary when you grow up?"

"No, sir," replied the boy. "I just want to know if you've got any foreign stamps."

A Swede was urged by friends to give up the idea of returning for a second term as a missionary to India, because it was so hot there. "Man," they urged him, "it's one hundred and twenty degrees in the shade!"

"Well," said the Swede, "we don't always have to stay in the shade, do we?"

A group on a home missions tour of Texas discovered they were lost. One member complained to the guide, "You told us you were the best guide in Texas."

"I am," the guide replied, "but now we're in Mexico."

An emcee at a banquet asked a friend to entertain the African sitting next to him. The friend wondered how he would communicate with the African. So, when food came, he said to him, "Yum, yum, yum—good, eh?"

When the coffee came, he said, "Glug, glug, glug—good, eh?"

When it came time for the message, to the friend's amazement the African was called up front as the distinguished guest speaker for the occasion. He gave a brilliant address. He had been won through missionaries, and educated at Oxford University. His English was flawless.

After great applause he returned to his seat. Turning to the friend, he said, "Blah, blah, blah—good, eh?"

During a visit to a mission field an American pastor spoke through an interpreter. The pastor told a rather lengthy story. At the end the congregation laughed. Since the interpreter had said only a few words, the pastor commented, "You sure translated that story fast."

"Yes," replied the interpreter, "your story was too long to explain, so I said, 'The pastor told a joke. Everyone, please laugh.'"

Old missionaries in the orient don't fade away—they become disoriented.

Money

BURGLAR *(in the parsonage):* If you move, you're a dead man. I'm looking for money.

PASTOR: Just let me get up and use my flashlight. I'll be glad to assist you in your search.

After figuring out his taxes a bewildered man exclaimed, "I'm overcome at the outcome of my income."

A man decided how much he would give his church this way. On cashing his paycheck he would throw the bills into the air and say, "Lord, you take what's yours, and whatever comes down will be mine."

A roofing salesman climaxed his pitch with, "Yes, sir! You only put down a tiny deposit, then you don't pay another penny for six months!"

To which the surprised deacon's wife demanded, "Who told you about us?"

A beleaguered father looked at his monthly bills and commented, "My entire salary runs into five figures—my wife's and my four daughters'."

While a man was hospitalized with a heart attack, his rich uncle died, leaving him a million dollars. The family, wishing to break the news without unduly exciting the patient, enlisted the help of the pastor. Gradually leading up to the point, the pastor asked the patient what he would do if he ever inherited a million dollars.

He replied, "I'd give half to the church." Whereupon the preacher had a heart attack.

During a violent snowstorm in the Rockies, a Red Cross rescue team flew by helicopter to within a mile of a mountain cabin all but covered by deep snowdrifts.

The rescuers struggled by foot through the deep drifts till they finally reached the cabin. Shoveling their way to the door, they knocked. When their summons was answered by a mountaineer, one rescuer said, "We're from the Red Cross."

"Well," said the mountaineer, scratching his head, "it's been a tough winter, and I don't see how we can give anything this year."

CHURCH TREASURER: It seems quaint that our ancestors used clamshells and beads for money.

ASSISTANT TREASURER: I wonder what they'd think of a wallet full of little plastic cards.

A miser said that he didn't believe the old saying, "You can't take it with you." At his death he left his estate of eight hundred thousand dollars to be divided equally between his two close friends. However, in his will he asked them to each place his share of four hundred thousand dollars in an envelope in cash, and to throw the envelope into the grave just before his coffin was covered with dirt.

At the graveside funeral, each threw in his envelope. Later, one of them confessed that hating to see all that money buried uselessly in the ground, he had kept out three hundred and fifty thousand dollars for a good cause, enclosing only fifty thousand dollars in his envelope.

The other expressed great shock. "Keeping that money was shameful. I threw in my personal check for my full amount."

Most churches accept all denominations —especially fifties and hundreds.

A fine is a tax for having done wrong. A tax is a fine for having done well.

If your outgo exceeds your inflow,
Then your upkeep will be your downfall.

PASTOR: How should we go about winterizing our camp dormitory?

TREASURER: First, I'd summerize the cost.

A miser is a person
  who gets his money the hoard way
  who thinks the world owes him a giving
  who picks up a check only when it's
      made out to him
  who, when it comes to picking up
      a dinner check, has an impediment
      in his reach.

Mothers and Daughters

LINDA SUE *(to little* FRIEND *visiting her house to watch TV):* We're going to have company for dinner tonight.
FRIEND: How do you know?
LINDA SUE: Mommy is putting the knives and forks on straight.

The five-year-old daughter of a missionary complained when she was served vegetable soup. "I like only chicken-noodle soup."

"Then pretend it's chicken noodle," her mother replied.

"Okay," the daughter said. "I'll pretend I'm eating it, too!"

PASTOR: Didn't Mrs. Brown look pleased when I told her she didn't look a day older than her daughter?
PASTOR'S WIFE: I really didn't notice. I was too busy watching the expression on her daughter's face.

MOTHER *(day after daughter left for college):* I lost a daughter but I gained a closet.

A mother often says to a restless child, "Sit still," while God says, "Wiggle."

A mother was trying to get the ketchup out of the bottle, so she kept smacking it. When the doorbell rang, her little girl greeted the minister, "Mother's in the kitchen hitting the bottle."

A primary Sunday school teacher showed her class a magnet and how it drew things to itself. Later, to test their listening ability she asked, "My name starts with *m* and I pick up things. What am I?"

A chorus of children hollered out, "Mother!"

A mother and daughter were washing dishes in the kitchen, while the father and his little son were watching TV in the den. Suddenly came a crash followed by complete, prolonged silence.

The son looked knowingly at his father and said, "It was Mom."

"How do you know?" the father asked.

The boy replied, "She didn't say anything!"

Music (Choir)

A little girl, visiting a large church for the first time, was surprised to see the choir members march into the choir loft wearing robes. She whispered to her mother, "They're not all going to preach, are they?"

FIRST CHOIR MEMBER: What kind of music do you hear in a shoe store?
SECOND CHOIR MEMBER: Sole music.

In a church with a high choir loft the song leader announced just before the sermon, "We'll sing, 'When we all get to heaven,' while the choir is going down."

The choir conductor was terribly frustrated because at each rehearsal at least one of the soloists with an important part was absent. At the final afternoon rehearsal, just a few hours before the major, well-publicized evening concert, the conductor thanked the organist for never having missed a practice session.

"Well, it's the least I could do," commented the organist, "considering that I won't be able to play at the concert tonight."

A man, with a realistic view of his talents, was asked to sing in the choir.

He replied, "I'm a tenor."

"That's fine," responded the choir leader warmly.

The man continued, "Ten or twelve notes off-key."

MOTHER: Whatever are you children playing?
CHILDREN: Church.
MOTHER: But people shouldn't whisper in church.
CHILDREN: We know, Mother, but we're in the choir!

After a pompous, overconfident newcomer had an audition for the choir, the minister of music gave his evaluation to the pastor. "He should be a tenor. Ten or eleven miles away from the choir."

Music (Loud)

Two older members were talking. The first one said, "It bothered me when young people brought their guitars into the church."

The second one said, "That didn't disturb me so much, but what did was when they plugged the guitars into the wall."

WOMAN TO ORGANIST: Your preludes are so loud I can't hear what my friends are saying.

After listening to an evening of rock performers, a choir director made the following report to his church's music committee: "Regardless of how we feel about rock music, we have to admit that it has opened up a whole new field of expression for kids who can't sing."

Eastern proverb: "If thine enemy wrong thee, give each of his children a drum."

Nature

When a mother saw a thunderstorm forming in midafternoon, she worried about her seven-year-old daughter who would be walking the three blocks from school to home. Deciding to meet her, the mother saw her walking nonchalantly along, stopping to smile whenever lightning flashed.

Glimpsing her mother, the little girl ran to her, explaining enthusiastically, "All the way home, God's been taking my picture!"

"Who put the stars in the sky?" asked the Sunday school teacher, reviewing the previous week's lesson.

"I know," said Johnny. "It was America."

"Why do you say it was America?" asked the surprised teacher.

"A lady sang about it in church," Jimmy explained. "You know the song that goes, 'It took America to put the stars in place!'"

Spring: When the whole countryside goes on releaf.

One evening when the moon was just a sliver in the sky, a four-year-old girl studied it, then exclaimed to her mother, "See—there's God's toenail."

A city resident was commenting to a farmer on the excellent crops of barley and corn, pointing out to him how grateful he should be to God for the sunshine, the rain, and the minerals in the ground.

After listening to the lengthy exhortation to thank God for his work in causing the barley and corn to grow, the farmer retaliated, "You should have seen the field when God had it by himself."

Newspaper Items

The Senior Department of the First Presbyterian Church will present *Hamlet* next Friday evening. No admission will be charged to see this tragedy in the church auditorium.

A minister, speaking to the local Rotary Club, told a number of excellent, clean jokes. Noticing the reporter for the local newspaper present, the minister begged him not to report any of the jokes in his article. "You see—I plan to use them before a number of different local audiences, and I don't wish them to get stale."

The reporter agreed. Picking up a newspaper the next day to read the report of his talk, the minister was startled to read, "The Reverend Jones also told several good jokes. Unfortunately, none of them can be repeated."

A newspaper, reporting the wedding of childhood sweethearts the previous Saturday in a local church, closed by saying, "So ended a friendship that began in school days."

Offering

A little boy fumbled around noisily in his pocket at offering time. His irritated mother asked, "Whatever are you looking for? You have your dime in your hand now."

"I'm looking for a quarter," said the lad. "If God is as good as the man on the platform says, then I'm raising his allowance."

During a sharing period in the early part of a service a visitor admitted a shortcoming. "I'm a spendthrift. I just cannot keep any money in my pocket. I give it away as if it grew on trees. Please pray for me."

"We certainly will," said the pastor, "right after the offering."

IRS (phoning a PASTOR): Do you have a member by the name of Archibald Normanski?

PASTOR: Yes, we do.

IRS: Did he make a gift of two thousand dollars to your church last year?

PASTOR: No, but call me tomorrow and he will have.

A family on vacation attended a church service with an unfamiliar order of worship. Two offerings were scheduled. As the offering plate was passed for a second time, a young son asked his father, "Is this for the sales tax?"

As the congregation departed from the morning service, a beggar, standing on the corner with outstretched hand, could be heard repeating, "Folks, it's just a one-time gift. No follow-up phone calls. No monthly pledges to meet."

A man joined a church. As far as the finance officials could figure out, he never gave a penny to the church. So the board asked the preacher to speak three times on the theme of giving. Still they could see no sign of any giving by this man.

So three board members, along with the pastor, called on him. When he understood the reason for their visit, he said, "You don't have the facts. Let me give some details. I have a mother in the hospital who just had a serious operation. Her hospital and doctors' bills amounted to several thousands of dollars.

"I have an uncle that had a stroke, and he's in an expensive nursing home.

"I have a son in an Ivy League college where the tuition is sky-high."

He named several other costly areas, then added. "Now, if I haven't given any of them one single penny, why should I give the church anything?"

Just before the offering the pastor announced, "The ushers will now pass the plate to the pay-rishioners."

A pastor was asking for gifts for urgently needed repairs on the sanctuary ceiling. After a pause Deacon Tight stood up, "I'll give ten dollars."

Just then a piece of plaster fell from the ceiling and hit the deacon on the head. A little stunned, Deacon Tight looked around and said, "Well, I guess I'd better give twenty dollars."

Then the pastor, looking upward, said, "Oh, Lord, hit him again."

Two members of different congregations were comparing their ministers. The first one said, "Ours is so interested in the flock."

To which the other retorted, "And ours in the fleece."

Taking a look at the offering in the collection plates which the ushers had just piled up neatly on the table in front of the pulpit, a minister preceded his sermon with this comment, "Sometimes I get the impression that you think this church is coin-operated."

A preacher who emphasized the point that salvation is as free as the water we drink was obliged to announce that the collection was pitifully small that day.

A parishioner stood to remind the minister of his statement that salvation is as free as water.

"Indeed it is," countered the preacher, "but when we pipe it to you, you have to pay for the plumbing."

"Roasted at the 1989 annual banquet of the Religious News Writers Association because of his fund-raising efforts, Dr. Jerry Falwell responded by recalling a letter proposing that his tombstone be inscribed with these words from Luke 16:22, "And it came to pass, that the beggar died.""

If you find that a dollar still goes as far as it used to, that means you are in church.

Your giving gives you away—you write your autobiography in your checkbook.

Church sign: SINCE YOU CAN'T TAKE IT WITH YOU, WHY NOT LEAVE IT HERE?

A preacher announced the offering. As the ushers marched forward to get the plates, the preacher commented, "Let us remember—that which we render unto God is deductible from that which we render unto Caesar."

Old Age (Health)

A young lady asked an elderly man, "Do you take part in any sports?"

He replied, "My parents won't let me."

Noting her surprise, he continued, "Yes, Mother Nature and Father Time."

MIDDLE-AGED WOMAN: How do you know when you're getting old?

ELDERLY WOMAN: When you stoop down to pick something up, and you say, "Is there anything else I can do while I'm down here?"

Two ladies were chatting in a department store. The first was telling her friend about her many ailments. "I've got rheumatoid arthritis. And my ankle is sprained. Also I'm short of breath. I can hardly swallow, and besides that there's a constant buzzing in my ears."

"Oh, my," said her friend, "you sure must be healthy to be able to stand all that pain."

Two old friends met after many years. "So many things have happened," said one. "I've had my teeth out, and a stove and refrigerator put in."

At a church social two middle-aged members were talking about the retired pastor, who happened to be sitting a few seats away. "He's failing somewhat," said one.

"Yes," added the other, "he seems to be losing his pep."

They were surprised when the pastor turned in his chair and said, "Yes, and they also say he's getting hard of hearing."

A group of senior citizens, attending a lecture, heard a speaker lash out at their enemies. He concluded, "The time has come when we must get rid of socialism and communism and anarchism and . . ."

At this point a little lady jumped to her feet and shouted, "And while we're at it, let's get rid of rheumatism, too!"

Two women in a supermarket met in the health-food section. Said one, "I think I'll go on a health-food diet."

"Not me," replied the other. "At my age I need all the preservatives I can get."

A broadcaster opened his daily program to shut-ins, "Welcome to Morning Medications."

Old Age (Memory)

"Who's absent-minded now?" the old deacon gleefully asked his wife, as they walked home from church. "You left your umbrella in the rack, but I remembered both mine and yours." He proudly showed her the two umbrellas.

"But," said his wife, "neither of us brought an umbrella today."

At the church's senior citizen's dinner the speaker began, "There are many advantages to growing old." After a pause he added, "But I can't think of any now."

A lady said to her pastor on leaving church. "I can't begin to tell you how much your sermons have meant to my husband since he lost his mind two years ago."

PARISHIONER: It's really disturbing. I can't always remember the street I live on.

COUNSELOR: Don't worry. It's probably just a mental block.

Optimism

A farmer who always saw the bright side of things enjoyed a sunny day. His gloomy neighbor would comment, "That sun will wither the crops."

Hunting together, they shot some ducks that landed on a pond. The optimist ordered his dog to get the ducks. Instead of swimming toward the ducks, the dog walked on top of the water, retrieved them, then brought them back to his master, still walking on top of the water.

"What do you think of that?" asked the optimist.

Replied the pessimist, "Your dog can't swim, can he?"

A pastor, coming to the church baseball game late and walking by left field, asked how the game was going.

"Fine," came the left fielder's answer.

"What's the score?" asked the pastor.

"They're winning eighteen to nothing," came the reply.

"Eighteen to nothing!" exclaimed the pastor. "Sounds more like a basketball game. How can you say things are going fine with a score like that?"

Came the answer, "Because we haven't come to bat yet."

An optimist is one who refuses to look at the world through woes-colored glasses.

An optimist is someone who picks out a shopping cart and expects all its wheels to go in the same direction at the same time.

An optimist is someone who drops a dollar in the offering plate and expects a hundred-dollar sermon.

People who say that something is impossible should not interrupt those who are managing to get it done.

A doctor had piped-in music installed in his office. Treating a woman patient, he was telling her that she would have to lose at least forty pounds, when over the loudspeaker came "The Impossible Dream."

Pastors (Anniversaries)

On a pastor's first anniversary a church gave him a new Bible. On his second year they gave him a new clock. On his third, a new typewriter. On his fourth anniversary they gave him a new set of matching luggage.

When the new minister was introduced, the applause was loud and long. He thanked them, and said that he hoped to be with them many years and celebrate many anniversaries. Again much clapping. Then he added, "When there's applause at the start of a pastor's ministry, that's faith; in the middle, that's hope; and at the end, that's charity."

Pastors (Duty)

The true task of a pastor is to comfort the disturbed, and to disturb the comfortable.

As the family drove home from church, their small son said, "I'm going to be a minister when I grow up."

"Wonderful," said his mother. "What made you decide you want to be a preacher?"

"Well," replied the boy thoughtfully, "I'll have to go to church on Sunday anyway. And I think it would be more fun to stand up and shout than to sit still and listen."

An American preacher, visiting a church in Germany, was asked by the local pastor to say a few words of greeting. When finished, he said, "Now I'll turn you back to your German shepherd."

PASTOR *to his little* DAUGHTER: What did that visitor say to you at the end of the service?

DAUGHTER: Oh, he just wanted to know if you were the pastor of this church. I told him that you were the present encumbrance.

The difference between a preacher and a congregation is that the minister is paid for being good, whereas the congregation is good for nothing.

Pastors (Marksmanship)

"Is the new minister a good shot?" a hunter asked a fellow member of the church, who had taken the new pastor out hunting.

The member reflected for a moment. It was strictly against his principles to speak a disparaging word about a man of the cloth. Finally he made his response, "Yes, a fine shot he is—but it's marvelous how the Lord protects the birds when he's shooting!"

RECTOR *(on phone to his BISHOP):* I just heard that the rector of our largest cathedral has died. May I take his place?

BISHOP: It's all right with me, if it's all right with the undertaker.

Pastors (Relaxation)

A pastor, still tired from a busy Sunday, fell asleep watching the Monday-night football game. He slept through the rest of the game, and through the rest of the night, in front of the TV set.

Next morning his wife, worried lest he miss the men's prayer breakfast, shook him awake, calling, "Dear, its twenty to seven!"

"In whose favor?" he asked.

LITTLE BOY: Mom, why does the pastor get a month's vacation when my daddy only gets two weeks?

MOM: Well, Son, if he's a good pastor, he needs it. If he isn't, the congregation needs it.

Pastors (Tact)

The pastor's family was given a mince pie for Christmas by a parishioner who was a devoted friend but a very poor cook. The pie was dry and overspiced. The pastor's wife had to throw it out.

Meeting the parishioner at church next Sunday, the pastor, realizing that he would have to say something about the pie, finally blurted out, "We appreciate your thoughtfulness, and let me assure you that mince pie like yours never lasts long at our house."

Pastors (Trouble)

A minister was busy nailing up a trailing vine. A boy stood by watching for a long time. Finally, the minister smiled and said, "Well, my young friend, are you trying to get a hint or two on gardening?"

"No, sir," said the boy, "I'm just waiting to hear what a minister says when he hammers his thumb."

A new pastor went into his office just in time to meet the former pastor, who was clearing out his desk. The former pastor wished the new pastor his best, then said, "I have two letters hidden away in the vault in case things don't go so well for you. If after a year attendances and offerings are down, take out letter number one and read it. If after two years things are still bad, then read letter two."

A year went by. Things were not going well. Attendances were down, as were offerings. So just before the annual church meeting the new pastor, fearful lest he be fired, took out letter one. Opening it, he noted the advice that he should blame the former pastor, saying things had been so bad on arrival that he couldn't correct them in a year. The letter advised him to ask for another year.

It worked. He stayed a second year. But again toward the annual meeting attendances were lower than ever, and giving poorer too. So the night before the annual meeting the pastor took out letter two. Opening it, he read, "Write two quick letters."

An overwrought pastor was seen going daily to a railway track to watch an express train streak by. A friend asked, "Pastor, why do you come here every day to see the Conrail flyer go by?"

"Because," retorted the pastor, "I like to see something I don't have to push."

A new kind of chain letter has been circulating these days among churches. This chain letter asks for no money. Instead you send a copy of the letter to six other churches that are tired of their ministers. Then you bundle up your pastor and ship him to the church at the bottom of the list. In one week you will receive 16,436 ministers, one of which should be a dandy. But beware—one church broke the chain and got its old pastor back!

A pastor who was experiencing serious trouble with his board said he slept like a baby. He explained, "I sleep for an hour. Then I wake up and cry for an hour. Then I sleep a while, and then wake up and cry a while. And I do this all night long!"

Pastors (Young)

A young pastor, fresh out of seminary and city-bred, was visiting one of his parishioners, a farmer. Pointing to a field, the pastor commented, "That wheat field doesn't look so good. I'd be surprised if you get five bushels an acre."

"So would I," replied the farmer. "That's my corn field."

A long-time member learned that his church had called a young man, just out of seminary, as its new pastor. "He will bring new ideas and a fresh approach to the congregation," his informer added.

The old-timer commented, "Guess we're moving to greener pastures."

A young pastor, speaking for the first time in a jail service, began, "I'm so glad to see so many of you here today."

Patience

FIRST PREACHER: How do you preach patience to people and make it effective?

SECOND PREACHER: By making the sermon so long that they have to practice it while they listen.

A mother thanked God in a testimony service for the blessing of her four healthy, lively sons. Then she added, "And I'm asking God for patience to endure my blessings."

A prayer: "Give me patience, and give it to me immediately."

Patience is that quality that is needed just as it is exhausted.

The really happy and patient person is one who can enjoy the scenery when on a detour.

Peace

WOMAN: My father fought in World War II. My grandfather fought in World War I. My great-grandfather fought in the Spanish-American War and my great-great-grandfather fought in Napoleon's army.

NEIGHBOR: Can't your people get along with anybody?

A Western visitor to a Moscow zoo was amazed to see a cage marked CO-EXISTENCE, containing a lion and some lambs.

"How in the world do you do it?" the visitor asked.

"Nothing to it," replied the Russian zookeeper. "We just add a fresh lamb now and then."

A shipwrecked sailor, after three years of quiet on a deserted island, jumped for joy when one day a ship anchored in the harbor.

An officer, coming ashore in a small boat, handed the sailor a bunch of newspapers, saying, "The captain suggests that you read what's going on in the world before you decide whether or not you wish to be rescued."

As the hunter pointed his rifle at the bear, the bear called out, "Can't we talk this over like two intelligent, civilized beings?"

The hunter lowered his gun. "What do you want to talk over?"

The bear replied, "Why do you want to shoot me?"

"Simple," grunted the hunter, "I want a fur coat."

"All I want is a good breakfast," said the bear, smiling.

So they sat down—real close—to work out an agreement. After a while the bear rose to his feet—all alone. They had reached a compromise. The bear had secured his breakfast, and the hunter was inside a fur coat.

Plagiarism

The teacher of the men's class used a lot of material from other sources without giving credit. He defended himself by saying, "All work and no plagiarism makes me a dull teacher."

A preacher, accused of using the materials of other preachers, defended himself. "When their hog goes through my grinder, it's my sausage."

Someone remarked, "Maybe it's baloney."

Plagiarism is stealing a ride on someone else's train of thought.

"What I have to say in my sermon today," a preacher began, "I will say in a few appropriated words."

Some sermons may be both original and good. The original parts may not be good, and the good parts may not be original.

Prayer

The ship was sinking rapidly. The captain called out, "Anyone here know how to pray?"

A man stepped forward.

"Good," exclaimed the captain. "You pray. The rest of us will put on the life preservers. We're one short."

A pastor warned his congregation against going overboard in requests to God, against always saying, "Give me." He summed it up: "Don't put all your begs in one ask it."

Bill Moyers, when special assistant to President Lyndon Johnson, was asked to say grace at a family meal in the White House. As Moyers prayed softly, the president said, "Speak up."

Moyers looked up, "I wasn't praying to you, Mr. President."

Prayer, for many, is a message sent up to God at night and on Sundays when the rates are cheaper.

An employee was found asleep on the job by his supervisor. After a severe tongue lashing, the employee cried out in indignation, "Can't a man even close his eyes for a few minutes of silent prayer?"

Starting the day with a devotional period of Bible reading and prayer will keep us from being a surly riser.

Procrastination

YOUNG SON: What does "procrastinate" mean?
FATHER: I'll tell you later.

Noah didn't wait for it to rain before
he started building the ark.

References

A professor, frustrated with the hazard of writing letters of recommendation for people with dubious qualifications, composed some statements that can be read two ways.

For example, to describe someone totally incapable: "I most heartily recommend this candidate with no qualifications whatsoever."

To describe an unproductive applicant: "I am sure that no person would be better for the job."

To describe a zealous incompetent: "He'd like to work for you in the worst possible way."

To fit loafers: "You will be very fortunate to get this person to work for you."

After looking through some papers, a personnel manager said to a prospective employee: "I see you have references from three ministers. Since we don't work on Sundays in this office, do you think you could supply a reference from someone who sees you on weekdays?"

Retirement

An efficiency expert, studying a company's policies, asked, "How many of your employees are headed for retirement?"

Came the answer, "One hundred percent. We have no one going the other way."

Two retired church elders on a cruise sat beside each other one lunchtime. One asked, "Where did you go last year?"

The other answered, "We took a cruise around the world. Next year we'll try someplace else."

Some folks who retired to a hilltop in South Dakota named it "Mount Rush-No-More."

It takes retirement to reveal the joy of work.

Retirement is that time of life when you know all the answers—but nobody bothers to ask you the questions.

Secretaries

The bishop acquired a new secretary, a former Pentagon employee. She immediately reorganized the diocesan filing system, labeling one file cabinet SACRED and the other TOP SACRED.

DENOMINATIONAL EXECUTIVE: My wife isn't jealous. She doesn't care how good-looking my secretary is as long as he's efficient.

A secretary decided to apply for work in a church office. She filled out a job application and later was interviewed by the pastor.

The pastor noted that she didn't fill in the year of her birth. "I see that your birthday is July tenth," said the pastor. "May I ask what year?"

"Every year," replied the secretary.

A missionary doctor had a secretary-helper who had trouble reading the doctor's handwritten notes on the various cases. One day, after a patient had left the doctor's office, she was handed a piece of paper which after some frustration she finally figured out as saying, "Shot in the lumbar region." So she carefully typed on the patient's permanent record card, "Wounded in the woods."

A denominational headquarters office hired a new secretary. After a late arrival every day for a week, the boss said to her one morning, "You're thirty minutes late again. Do you know what time we start work in this office?"

The secretary replied, "No, sir. They're always working when I get here."

Self-Centeredness

A woman answered the door to find a man taking up a collection for an impoverished widow down the block. "She's low on food, clothes, and about to be thrown out into the bitter cold because she's four months behind on her rent."

"Oh, my," said the woman "how blessed she is to have found such a good Samaritan. Who are you?"

"I," said the good Samaritan, "am her landlord."

Two little children, brother and sister, were visiting their grandmother. She put two apples on the table, one large, red, and juicy, and the other small and half-ripe.

"Now, sweeties," she said, "I want to see which of you has the better manners."

"She does," said the little boy, taking the large, red, juicy apple.

This is an often-told story of a modern Job. This poor man's business was ruined. His son was killed in a car accident. He was mugged by robbers and suffered a broken jaw. The doctor told him he had an incurable disease. To top it all, his wife left him.

Reciting this list of woes to a friend, he expected a little sympathy, to say the least. Instead, as he unfolded each wretched detail, his friend commented, "But it could have been worse."

Finally, the unfortunate man screamed, "What do you mean—*it could have been worse?*"

The friend immediately replied, "It could have happened to me."

Two men in the wilderness saw bear tracks. One began putting on running shoes.

The other said, "What good are running shoes. You cannot outrun a bear."

"No," replied the first man as he laced up his shoes, "but I can outrun you."

It's always easier to find the silver lining in someone else's cloud.

Isn't it strange how faraway earthquakes, floods, tornadoes, hurricanes, and wars seem less disastrous than the first scratch on your new car?

MOTHER: I wish you two wouldn't argue all the time. Why can't you agree?

KAREN: We do. Steve wants the biggest piece of pie, and so do I!

From a window a mother was watching her two small sons enjoy the first snowfall of the season. Sensing something unfair, she opened the window and called out, "Johnny, why don't you let your little brother have his turn with your sled part of the time."

Johnny hollered back, "I do, Mother. I take it going downhill, and he has it going up."

Sermons (Good)

Wherever a preacher went, one of his members followed him, even to a jail service, a nursing-home Bible study, and a rescue-mission assignment.

When asked why this desire to hear his pastor on every occasion, he replied, "I heard that every preacher has one good sermon, and I don't want to miss it."

FIRST MEMBER: That sermon sure got to me. It pricked my conscience.

SECOND MEMBER: I can see how it would. I thought it had some good points.

A lady said to her pastor, "Your sermons are so good they ought to be published."

The preacher, trying to be modest, said, "Posthumously, you mean?"

"Yes, and the sooner the better."

Sermons (Long)

A man, trying to find a church for the first time, arrived while the pastor was preaching. "Is the sermon over yet?" he asked.

The usher at the door replied, "Yes, but the preacher doesn't know it."

One warm, sunny day a pastor announced to his congregation, "My beloved, I have here in my hands two sermons: a thousand-dollar sermon that lasts ten minutes, and a hundred-dollar sermon that lasts one hour. Now we'll take up the offering and see which one you want me to deliver."

A pastor announced that the offering would be taken at the end of the service. A little boy fidgeted restlessly as the sermon seemed to drag on and on. Finally, he leaned over and whispered to his mother, "Do you think he'd let us go if we give him the money now?"

A guest preacher said that before giving his message he had determined to be three things: to be clear, to be brief, and to be seated.

A homiletics professor told his class of budding preachers to remember the five B's as one sure sign of a good sermon, "Be brief, brother, be brief."

FIRST MEMBER: What's the difference between a preacher and an author?

SECOND MEMBER: You can shut up an author by closing a book.

If all the people who sit through long sermons were lined up three feet apart—they would stretch.

An admiring member of the congregation said to the pastor at the door after the service, "A fine sermon indeed, and well-timed too."

Another member, overhearing the remark, chirped up, "It certainly was well-timed. Half the congregation had their watches out."

A subject may not be exhausted by a long sermon, while the congregation is.

Sermons (Poor)

A lady noticed that every Monday morning her pastor drove down to a restaurant by the river where he met with three or four men. After several weeks of the same ritual, curiosity got the better of her, so she asked him what he was doing.

The pastor replied, "Those men are pastors from other churches nearby, and we've been meeting every Monday morning to exchange sermons."

"Oh, pastor," she replied, "don't do that. You always get the worst of the bargain."

A mother who had to stay home from church to look after a new baby asked her little son, "What did the preacher preach about this morning?"

The little lad thought for a moment, then answered, "He didn't say."

A wit commented on a certain preacher's rambling sermon, "If his text had had the measles, his sermon would never have caught the disease."

A well-meaning woman said to her minister after the service, "Despite what people say, I like your sermons."

NEIGHBOR: Does your Sunday morning service usually start on time?

CHURCH MEMBER: Yes, our service starts at eleven sharp and ends at twelve dull.

A minister, suddenly called away over a weekend, asked his new assistant to take the service. Returning home, he asked his wife how she thought the assistant did, and especially about his sermon.

"He conducted the service very well," his wife responded, then added, "I don't like to say it, but his sermon was one of the poorest I've ever heard. Didn't seem logical. Didn't make sense."

In the office later that day, the minister saw his assistant and asked him how his sermon had gone.

"Fine, sir. Absolutely wonderful. I didn't have time to prepare anything new myself, so I preached one of your old sermons."

A guest minister stayed overnight in a small town after filling the pulpit of the town's only church the day before. In the morning he dropped into a hardware store.

Recognizing him, a boy exclaimed, "Weren't you the preacher yesterday?"

Expecting a compliment, the preacher with a smile said, "Yes."

The boy blurted out, "That was the worst sermon I ever heard."

A member of the congregation, standing near, said, "Don't pay any attention to that boy. He's not very bright. He just repeats everything he hears everyone else saying."

His sermons are sound advice—99 percent sound, and 1 percent advice.

An evangelist, haggling to get a better price on an item from the antique dealer, pleaded, "You know, I'm just a poor preacher."

The dealer replied, "Yes, how well I know. I heard you preach last night."

The soloist stood to sing. As the piano accompaniment began, she said, "Before I sing, I'd like to express my appreciation to the pastor. It's his sermons that have taught me the truth of this song 'Wasted Years.'"

As a preacher droned on and on, the laymen in charge of the service threw the gavel at the preacher. Missing the preacher, the gavel hit a woman in the front row. Before she lapsed into unconsciousness, she was heard to whisper, "Hit me again. I can still hear him."

Pastors could learn from the cross-eyed discus thrower, who though he didn't win many prizes, sure kept the attention of all the spectators in the stands.

He's like a ship. He toots loudest when in a fog.

He gives you in length what he lacks in depth.

His sermons are like the horns of a steer, a point here, and a point there, and a lot of bull in between.

He doesn't put enough fire into his sermons. It would be better if he put his sermons into the fire.

Loud-speaking systems amplify a preacher's voice but not his ideas.

The preacher who doesn't strike oil in fifteen minutes should stop boring.

He gives a moving speech. Long before he's finished his congregation wants to move out of the sanctuary.

Many a preacher begins by not knowing what he's going to say, and ends by not knowing what he's said.

One scientist took sixteen years to discover helium. Another took thirty years to find radium. But many preachers take only ten minutes to produce tedium.

Sermons (Preparation)

A young minister frequently boasted in public that all the time he needed to prepare his Sunday morning sermon was the few minutes it took him to walk to the church from the parsonage next door.

Soon after, the elders bought him a new parsonage five miles away.

At a Wheaton (Illinois) College chapel service a speaker was preaching from his notes. He turned a page over when he was finished with it and let it drop over the side of the pulpit down onto the platform floor. Moments later he would release another page and so on.

Those sitting in the balcony near the front had a good view of what was happening, for they were looking right down on the pulpit.

As the preacher threw down the last page, he said, "I could go on and on. I wish I had the time to do so."

"Oh, no, you can't," came a voice from the balcony. "You just ran out of stuff."

MINISTER (TO WIFE): Well, Mrs. X is moving away next week. I'll be sorry to see her go.

WIFE: You'll be sorry to see her go? Why, she's been the worst member of your congregation!

MINISTER: True—but she's given me material for a lot of great sermons!

Sexton

Trying to catch a church mouse, a sexton ran out of cheese. So he put a picture of cheese in a mousetrap.

Looking in the mousetrap the next morning, he saw that he had caught a picture of a mouse.

SEXTON: I've seen ten ministers come and go, but I still believe in God.

Sleeping in Church

A scientist made a careful study of people who fell asleep in church. His conclusion was that if all the sleeping congregants were laid end to end, they would be a lot more comfortable.

A seminary student found out how dull his sermon was when he asked a classmate what he thought of the sermon's train of thought.

Came the startling answer, "Your train lacked nothing but a sleeping car."

Thinking others might have received a different impression, he asked another student to suggest a closing prayer befitting the sermon. Came the equally shocking answer, "Now I lay me down to sleep."

A minister asked his wife at the dinner table, "Did you think the congregation reacted favorably to my sermon this morning?"

"I'm sure of it," replied his wife, "for I saw several nodding at the same time."

Blessed are they that blink, for they shall soon enter the Land of Nod.

Sermons affect people in different ways. Some rise to leave, greatly strengthened, while others awake, greatly refreshed.

Spoonerisms

Rev. William Archibald Spooner, learned Anglican clergyman and warden of New College, Oxford, suffered from something scientists would later call "metathesis," the accidental transposition of letters of syllables in the words in a sentence. More popularly, this practice came to be known as "spoonerism."

Here is a sampling of some of his reported, better-known spoonerisms.

Standing in his pulpit, he would say, "The Lord is a shoving leopard." His congregation would understand that he meant to say, "The Lord is a loving shepherd."

He once told a nervous bridegroom, "It is kisstomery to cuss the bride."

He would announce the next hymn as "Kinkering Congs Their Tattles Tike." And everyone turned to "Conquering Kings Their Titles Take."

Almost everyone has heard of his remark when directing a woman to her seat, "Mardon me, padam, but this pie is occupued. Allow me to sew you to another sheet."

Calling on the dean of a large cathedral, Spooner asked the prelate's secretary, "Is the bean dizzy?"

He began a lecture to a group of farmers, "I have never before addressed so many tons of soil," meaning, of course, "sons of toil."

Before expelling a student he scolded him, "You have deliberately tasted two worms and can leave Oxford by the town drain."

He congratulated a friend who had just acquired a country cottage on his "nosy little cook."

When a student was absent from a class, he chided him, "You hissed my mystery lecture."

He referred to Queen Victoria as "Our queer old dean," instead of "dear old queen."

Living to be eighty-six years of age, he cheerily committed spoonerisms in public right to the end. When the soldiers came back from France after World War I, he told a crowd of patriots, "We'll have the hags flung out."

He praised a cyclist for having a "well-boiled icicle," and described a catastrophe as a "blushing crow."

Sunday School

BOY: Must have been lonely on Noah's ark!
SUNDAY SCHOOL TEACHER: Couldn't they have done a lot of fishing?
BOY: What—with two worms?

The teacher of an adult Sunday school group, who dressed very informally even for Sunday morning church service, remarked to his class during a lesson on the Book of Exodus, "I don't go along with this concept of dressing for success. Let's face it. Can anyone tell me what color necktie Moses was wearing when he parted the Red Sea?"

A little boy was enrolled in a Sunday school where the heat came through a register in the floor from the furnace in the cellar right below. After three unavoidable absences the little fellow said he didn't want to go back to Sunday school.

"Why not?" asked his mother.

"Because," the boy whimpered, "they're going to throw me into the furnace."

The puzzled parent talked to the Sunday school teacher, who in turn talked to the boy, who blurted out, "Didn't you say that after three absences you would drop people from the register?"

During a game at the Sunday school's annual picnic, the superintendent was struck on the head by a baseball. He was taken to the local hospital for X-rays and observation over the weekend.

Sunday morning the assistant superintendent announced, "The superintendent is resting comfortably. The X-rays of his head showed nothing."

SUNDAY SCHOOL TEACHER: What is an archangel?
PUPIL: One of the angels who came out of the ark.

A lad was asked by his Sunday school teacher to draw a picture of the holy family's flight into Egypt. So he pictured father, mother, baby, and a third adult. "That's Mary and Joseph and the babe," he explained.

When asked who the third adult was, he replied, "Oh, that's Pontius the Pilot."

Time

A group of students from Moody Bible Institute were conducting a service in Chicago's Cook County Jail. A young would-be preacher waxed eloquently, "Gentlemen, we don't know where we'll be in the future. We don't know where we'll be ten years from now. Even ten months from now. Where will you be ten minutes from now?"

From a corner of the cell a voice piped up, "We'll be right here, buddy."

Some people value time so poorly that it takes them two hours to watch "Sixty Minutes."

Two turtles decided to stop in a drugstore for a soda. Just as they were served their drink, it began to rain. "Go home and get the umbrella," said the big turtle.

"Okay," replied the little turtle, "but promise not to drink my soda."

Two years later the big turtle said to himself, "I guess he's never coming back. I may as well drink his soda."

Just then a voice called from the other side of the door, "If you touch that soda, I will not go home and get the umbrella."

A pastor so frequently used the expression "I see my time has gone" that his wife threatened to put it on his tombstone.

Tongue

A wife, walking out the door to visit her neighbor just before dinner, called to her husband, "I'll only be a minute. Don't forget to stir the stew every twenty minutes till I get back."

A wife complained to her husband about the bad manners of her new neighbor. "If that woman yawned once, Albert, while I was talking, she yawned a dozen times."

To which Albert replied, "Maybe she wasn't yawning, dear. Maybe she was trying to say something."

Did you hear about the physician who tried and tried to X-ray his patient's jawbone, but all he could get was a moving picture?

A husband objected to his wife's long phone calls. "She's the only person who can call 'Dial-a-Prayer' and engage it in conversation."

You don't have to be smart to say things that do.

She's always letting the chat out of the bag.

Some people keep secrets with telling effect.

There's nothing wrong in having nothing to say—unless you insist on saying it.

It's all right to hold a conversation, but you should let go of it now and then.

A rumor goes in one ear and out many mouths.

Travel

The youngsters were trying to talk their grandmother into taking her first airplane ride. "You fly through the air and get there so quick," they reasoned.

"Not me," the grandmother replied. "I don't go for all those new-fangled things. I'm going to sit right here and enjoy television like the Lord intended."

A new missionary was learning to operate a helicopter. When he was up six hundred feet, he came down suddenly.

Asked what happened, he replied, "Got chilly up there, so I turned off the fan."

A church group touring the Near East pulled to a stop. It was midafternoon. "Why are we stopping here?" asked one of the group.

"This is where Polycarp was burned at the stake," replied the tour leader.

"When did that happen?" asked the man.

"I think around one fifty," the tour guide responded.

Looking at his watch, the tour member turned to his wife, "We missed it by an hour."

Sign in a travel agency: IF YOU DON'T GO FIRST CLASS, YOUR HEIRS WILL.

When a lady entered a crowded bus, a man offered her his seat. She asked why he was doing it. He said, "I was taught to always offer my seat to a lady."

She replied, "I'm a person," and refused to take the seat.

He remarked, "Well, then, I'll sit here till the first lady comes along."

On a bumpy airplane flight a denominational executive became quite alarmed. His fears were intensified when he recalled the sign on a building in the airport he had just left—TERMINAL.

A church leader from Australia, making his first trip to the USA, flew on an Air New Zealand flight. Arriving at the Los Angeles terminal, he heard the loudspeaker announce an immediate departure for Oakland. Since this was his desired destination, he boarded the plane for the short hop north.

After take-off he thought it strange that the plane kept flying west over the ocean. After an hour he asked a stewardess where the plane was headed.

"Auckland," she replied.

The pilot of a four-engine jet announced over the intercom, "We'll be arriving a little late because an engine has conked out."

A second time, about a half-hour later, he made another announcement, "We'll be arriving even a little later because a second engine has conked out."

When a third time he announced that another engine had conked out, and that they would be delayed still longer, a passenger said to the fellow beside him, "If the fourth engine conks out, we'll be up here all night."

Tour group member at airport about to take off for ten days in the Holy Land: "How do you change a flat on the tire of a 747?"

Replied a second member: "You high-jack it."

A Sunday school teacher asked her class, "What do we learn from the story of Jonah?"

An eight-year-old put up his hand. "Travel by air," he said.

Ushers

A young usher, who had never before participated in a wedding, asked an arriving guest, "Are you a friend of the bride or groom?"

"I'm a friend of both," came the reply.

"I'm sorry, Madam," the youthful usher replied. "I'm afraid you'll have to choose a side. I haven't been told where to seat the neutrals."

A lady arrived at a church that was crowded every Sunday, too late for a seat. The usher offered her a seat on one of the stone steps of the choir loft.

Taking this as an insult, she walked away muttering, "If that's the way you treat visitors, no wonder the churches today are empty."

A boy of four was warned by his slightly older sister that he wouldn't be allowed to talk in church. "They just won't let you say a word," she said.

"Who won't?" the boy asked.

Came the reply, "The hushers!"

Vanity

A salesman sold so many pairs of ladies' shoes that the store manager had to place a special order to replenish the stock.

"How do you do it?" the manager demanded. "I hope you didn't mark down the prices."

"No, sir," the salesman explained. "I marked down the sizes."

A prominent socialite was outraged when the photographer showed her the proofs of some pictures she had recently posed for at his studio.

"Now I ask you," she yelled at the photographer, "do these pictures really look like me?"

Momentarily flustered, the photographer quickly regained his composure. "Madam," he said in a matter-of-fact tone, "the answer is in the negative."

Visitation

Some visitors stay longer in an hour than others do in a week.

A minister made a call on a parishioner, seriously ill in a hospital. Before taking his leave, he said, "Shall we have a word of prayer?"

He prayed for all people, all situations, and all the missionaries the church supported in various parts of the world.

When the "amen" was sounded, he turned to the weeping relative beside him, and said, "I hope your brother will soon be better."

To his surprise the sister replied, "Oh, he died while you were in China."

A lady who saw her minister coming up the front walk told her little girl what to tell him. When the knock came, the little girl opened the door.

"Is your mother home?" asked the minister.

The little girl replied, "No, Mummy isn't home. She went . . . she went. . . ." After an awkward pause, she turned toward the living room, and continued, "Mummy, where did you say you went?"

A New Jersey pastor who loved the out-of-doors owned a boat which he named *Visitation.* When anyone called the church when he was out on the boat, his secretary would say, "He's out on visitation."

On other afternoons when he was out playing golf, she would say, "Pastor has nine appointments this afternoon," meaning nine holes of golf to play.

A woman frequently visited by Jehovah's Witnesses asked friends what she could do to escape this annoyance.

A friend suggested buying an American flag, placing it inside her front door, and asking such callers to pledge allegiance before their spiel. "They will refuse to honor the flag," the friend said, "and your problem will be solved."

So the lady purchased an American flag and positioned it inside her front door. Two days later she spotted a visitor coming up her walk with her paraphernalia under her arm. Soon the bell rang.

When the lady of the house answered, the visitor asked for a few minutes of her time.

The lady of the house said, "You may, but first you must pledge allegiance to the flag."

The visitor pledged allegiance to the flag inside the door, then kept on talking, "In all my eighteen years as an Avon lady, this is the first time I've ever been asked to pledge allegiance to the flag!"

A Sunday school was taking a census of their community.

CENSUS-TAKER: Your name?

LADY OF THE HOUSE: Ann Jones.

CENSUS-TAKER: Your age, please?

LADY: Did the Hills next door give you their age?

CENSUS-TAKER: Yes, they did.

LADY: I'm the same age as they are.

CENSUS-TAKER: Very good. I'll write on the questionnaire, "Ann Jones is as old as the Hills."

PASTOR *(visiting a* YOUTH *hospitalized after a skiing accident):* You're a ski enthusiast. Would you say skiing is a colorful sport?

YOUTH: It most certainly is. You see white snow and Blue Cross.

A church visitor knocked on the door of a low-rent apartment house. The mother, spotting him coming, and not wishing to talk to the visitor, told her little boy to tell him that she was unable to come to the door because she was in the bathtub.

The son answered the door, "We don't have a bathtub, but Mom told me to tell you she's in it."

A pastor was phoned by a sick woman who was active in a church of another denomination, asking him if he would be kind enough to come to her home.

When he arrived, the pastor said to the lady's ten-year-old son, "I'm most happy your mother called me. Only tell me—is your minister out of town?"

"No, not at all," replied the little lad. "Mommy just said that she was afraid she might have a sickness that was contagious."

A pastor called on a home one afternoon after school. Suddenly a little boy rushed into the room, exhibiting a mangled, dead rat. As the mother let out a little shriek and shrank away, the little lad reassured her, "Oh, it can't hurt you. It's dead all right. I beat it and beat it until . . ." Then spotting the pastor, his tone changed to one of solemnity, " . . . until God called it home."

Wives

A man had his credit cards stolen on a trip to Hawaii. But he did not bother to report the theft.

When friends wondered why he didn't tell the police about his loss, he explained, "I find the thieves are charging far less on my credit cards than my wife ever did."

A man's wife had scratched the side of their new car as she backed it out of the garage.

"Don't worry about it," her husband said. "Those things happen. Take it to the body-repair shop and have it touched up."

As strange as it may seem, two weeks later she backed into a light pole and broke the right rear taillight. She was almost in tears when she told her husband about it.

"Don't worry about it" he said. "Take it to the body-repair shop and have it fixed."

"But," she said, "I'm so embarrassed to take it back there again."

"If you're embarrassed," he said, "just tell them that I did it."

"That's what is so embarrassing," she said. "I told them that the last time."

A bride brought a cake to the church social. Her mother-in-law, taking a bite, asked, "Joan, did you follow the recipe?"

"I sure did," said the bride. "Only I put in six eggs instead of four, because two were bad, and I wanted to even them up."

A pastor's wife said, "My husband wants me to wear my clothes longer—three years longer."

It is estimated that the average man speaks five thousand words a day, and that the average woman speaks seven thousand.

"The trouble is," complained one man, "when I come home from work, I've finished my five thousand, but my wife hasn't started her seven thousand yet."

A woman should try to make her husband feel as if he is the boss, even if he is only the chairman of the fund-raising committee.

A happy wife sometimes has the best husband, but more often makes the best of the husband she has.

A wife drove into a gas station and said to the attendant, "Fill him up."

Work

One man said, "Every morning I get up and look through the *Forbes* list of the richest people in America. If I'm not there, I go to work."

A patient told his doctor, "If there's anything wrong with me, Doctor, don't frighten me half to death by giving it a long, scientific name. Please, just tell me in plain English what's wrong."

"Well," replied the doctor hesitatingly, "to be perfectly frank, you're just plain lazy."

"Thanks, Doctor," muttered the patient. "Now I would appreciate it if you would give me the scientific name so I can tell my family."

"So you've been with the company forty years now, eh, Jones? And how long have you worked here?"

The president of a church men's group said to a prospective member, "Our organization is different. In most organizations half the members do all the work, and the other half does nothing. I am happy to say that in this organization, we do the exact opposite."

WIFE: How did it go at the office today?
HUSBAND: Terrible! The computer stopped, and we all had to think.

The personnel manager looked at the record of the applicant. "Looks like you've been fired from every job you've ever had."

The applicant retorted, "Yes, but you've got to admit—I'm no quitter."

COUNSELOR: How long have you worked for your present employer?
COUNSELEE: Ever since he threatened to fire me.

A lot of people who complain about being up to their ears in work are just lying down on the job.

For several days a farmer had been plowing with an ox and a mule together, working them rather hard. One morning the ox said to the mule, "Let's play sick today and maybe we can get some rest."

But the old mule said, "No, we need to get the work done before winter."

However, the ox played sick. The farmer brought him fresh hay and corn and made him feel comfortable as he looked the situation over.

When the mule came in all tired from plowing, the ox asked, "Did the farmer say anything about me?"

"Nothing," said the mule.

Next day the ox, thinking he had a good thing going, played sick again. At the end of the day he again asked the mule if the farmer had said anything about him.

"He didn't say anything to me directly," said the mule, "but he did stop downtown at the meat store and have a long talk with the butcher."

One reason a dollar doesn't do as much for people as it once did is that people won't do as much for a dollar as they once did.

Two things more difficult than work are looking for it, and trying to avoid it.

A loafer is a person who always looks forward to the yawn of the day.

A loafer is a fellow who has little longitude but much lassitude.

A loafer is a man whose wife is the power behind the drone.

Success is a matter of keeping on your toes and off other people's.

"Working mother"—that's a redundancy.

A loafer is a person who does his daily dozing.

If at first you do succeed —try something harder.

A loafer is a fellow who finds getting up each morning a tug-of-war between mind and mattress.

Works (Good)

A not-too-tidy housewife attended a women's weekend retreat and was revived spiritually. Arriving home, she told her husband, "Honey, we're going to sweep the country with these eternal truths!"

With minimum enthusiasm he replied, "I hope you start with the kitchen."

An important meeting of Anglican clergymen convened in London, England. After the bishop had called the meeting to order, the door opened and in came a rector obviously embarrassed by his late arrival. As he entered the room, he pulled out his pocket watch. In defensive tone and in loud voice he said to the bishop, "I have perfect faith in my watch."

The bishop replied in soft voice, "Sir, what you need is not perfect faith in your watch but good works."

Be nice to the fellows you meet on the way up, for they are the same fellows you will meet on your way down.

A dedicated worker in a Christian Service Brigade boys' club was putting in a cement walk. Suddenly two boys came around the corner, chasing a dog with a baseball in its mouth right across the freshly laid cement.

The man yelled at them fiercely.

Someone said, "I thought you liked boys."

"Yes," he replied, "but I like them in the abstract, not in concrete."

A Boy Scout, who had difficulty doing his daily good deed, told his church scoutmaster that finally he had succeeded that day.

"And what was your good deed for today?" asked the scoutmaster.

"Four of us helped a little old lady across a very busy street."

"Why four of you?"

"She didn't want to go."

A lady was being honored at a church banquet for her many activities at church, such as making uniforms for the baseball team, heading up the annual dinner, tutoring students, visiting the sick, taking flowers to the shut-ins, and for a host of other good deeds.

A visitor, who couldn't see the platform very well, turned to the woman next to her and asked what the honored woman looked like.

Came the answer, "Exhausted!"

STUDENT *(in Bible school):* Ever heard of the resolutions of the disciples?

FELLOW STUDENT: No, but I've heard a great deal about the Acts of the Apostles.

A husband installed an electric bell at his front door, connected the wires to a battery, and pressed the button. To his delight the bell rang out clearly.

Then he decided to get a light so people could see the doorbell. Buying the light, he attached the wires to the battery. But when he flicked the switch, to his chagrin, there was no light.

He enlisted the help of an electrician, who expressed surprise that the husband had connected both bell and light to the same battery, which, he explained, though powerful enough to ring a bell, could not also shine a light.

Exclaimed his wife, "I see—it takes a lot more power to shine than to shout!"

After all is said and done, there's much more being said than done.

Worry

A man worried and worried about everything, whether personal, national, or global. He even worried that he wasn't worrying enough.

As he worried, he sat and drank coffee, cup after cup. When he went to bed, he couldn't sleep. He just percolated.

Church visitor to constant worrier: "Don't let worry kill you. Let the church help."

Hypochondriac: One who can't leave well enough alone.

Worship

A Lutheran preacher was scheduled to preach in a church in another state. When it came time to speak, he clipped his microphone to his lapel. Unsure whether it was switched on, he tapped it gently, apparently with no result. So, leaning very close to it, he said in a loud whisper that echoed around the church, "There is something wrong with this microphone."

The well-trained and responsive congregation, very familiar with the latest in liturgical language, replied at once, "And also with you."

Zeal

A seminary student often spoke in evangelistic churches during the school year where it was customary to give an invitation to people to publicly respond to the gospel by raising their hands.

The next summer he took a job as lifeguard at an ocean beach. On his first day at the job, suddenly he noticed a commotion in the deep waters. A hand went up in distress.

Absentmindedly, the lifeguard stood up and said, "I see that hand. Is there another?"

Dwight D. Eisenhower: "What counts is not necessarily the size of the dog in the fight—it is the size of the fight in the dog."